URGENT PRAYERS

BLOOM AND INK LEGACY PRESS

URGENT PRAYERS

A Spirit-Led Guide to Breakthrough in Every Area of Life

Charma-Lee Ritchie

Scripture quotations are taken from the Holy Bible, New International
Version® (NIV®).
Copyright © 1973, 1978, 1984, 2011 by Biblica, Inc.™
Used by permission. All rights reserved worldwide.
ISBN: 979-8-218-83562-0

Cover Design: Charma-Lee Ritchie
Interior Design: Charma-Lee Ritchie
Publisher: Bloom and Ink Legacy Press

Disclaimer:
This book is intended as a spiritual prayer resource. It is not a substitute
for medical, psychological, legal, or professional advice. Readers facing
serious mental health, medical, or legal concerns are encouraged to seek
qualified professional assistance in addition to prayer.

"The prayer of a righteous person is powerful and effective."
 James 5:16 (NIV)

Dedication

This book is dedicated to my son, Richard, and to every soul who has whispered prayers in the dark, cried tears into a pillow, or lifted weary hands to heaven with no words left to say. To the single mother, the struggling father, the worried son, the grieving daughter, the discouraged worker, and the hurting believer, this is for you. May these prayers be your lifeline, your fire, your comfort, and your hope. With love and faith, Charma-Lee Ritchie

Acknowledgements

First and foremost, I give all glory, honor, and praise to God. Every word in these pages was born from His presence, shaped by His Spirit, and sustained by His grace. This book did not begin as a project or an idea, but as a quiet stirring in my heart, one that required obedience, faith, and courage to bring forth. There were moments when I doubted myself, moments when the weight of the message felt heavier than my strength, and moments when fear tried to silence what God had entrusted to me. Yet, time and time again, He reminded me that this work was never mine alone. Without His guidance, His patience, and His unfailing love, this book would not exist. It stands as a testimony to His faithfulness and His perfect timing.

I am deeply grateful to the precious people who surrounded me in prayer throughout this journey. To those who lifted my name before God when my own words felt insufficient, thank you. To those who stood quietly in faith, believing with me even when the path was unclear, thank you. Your prayers carried me through moments of weariness and uncertainty, reminding me that I was never walking alone. This book is not only the result of personal obedience, but of collective intercession, shared faith, and spiritual covering.

To my husband, Rodrick, thank you for the times you prayed for me, sometimes aloud, sometimes quietly, but always sincerely. Your prayers were a shield during seasons when battles felt overwhelming, and strength felt distant. In moments when I felt vulnerable or unsure, your support reminded me of God's care and protection. I am grateful for your willingness to stand beside me in faith, even when the process was not always easy or understood. Your prayers mattered more than you may ever realize.

To my son, Richard, thank you for standing in the gap with such boldness and compassion. Your prayers were filled with sincerity and trust in God's promises, and they reminded me that God's timing is always perfect. Watching you pray with confidence strengthened my own faith and encouraged me to remain steadfast. You are a constant reminder of God's goodness and purpose, and I love you more than words can express.; to Sherye Phillips Watson, Georgette Stewart-Harrisingh, Latoy, Lethoya Oliphant, Pastor Sean Anderson and family, thank you for your unwavering prayers and gentle encouragement. Each of you served as a steady anchor during times when I felt stretched, tired, or unsure. Your willingness to intercede on my behalf, to stand with me in faith, and to speak life when I struggled to find the words made a profound difference. Your prayers were not unnoticed, and your faithfulness will forever be etched into the foundation of this work.

To Mrs. Deloris Kellerman, lovingly known as Aunty Del, and her husband, Dr. Kellerman thank you for being a constant voice of faith and reassurance. Your words consistently pointed me back to God's promises and reminded me of the power of trust and perseverance. You spoke life into this journey when doubt tried to creep in, and your encouragement strengthened my resolve to continue. This book is as much yours as it is mine, because it was birthed within a community of prayer, faith, and unwavering belief. I pray that the Lord rewards you abundantly for every whispered prayer, every encouraging word, and every act of love you extended along the way.

To everyone who supported me through prayer, conversation, patience, and belief, thank you. This book is a reflection of what can be accomplished when faith is shared, burdens are carried together, and God remains at the center. My prayer is that these pages minister to hearts, strengthen faith, and remind every reader that they are never alone.

With heartfelt gratitude,

Charma-Lee Ritchie

TABLE OF CONTENTS

Dedication
Acknowledgements
Introduction: Why Urgent Prayers Matter

Introduction

Why Urgent Prayers Matter

Life does not wait. When trials come, they often arrive quickly and without warning. Bills pile up. Marriages strain. Children wander. Faith weakens. Even the strongest hearts can feel faint.

But God has given us a weapon, a gift, and a privilege, prayer.

Prayer is not empty words. It is a direct line to the throne room of heaven. These are not casual prayers; they are urgent prayers. They rise from the heart in desperation, faith, and expectation. They are personal, emotional, and Spirit-led.

This book was created to equip believers with prayers they can lift immediately in the middle of life's storms. Organized into ten parts covering home life, work, parenting, faith, healing, and restoration, these prayers are meant to be spoken, declared, and believed.

Pray them aloud. Make them your own. Insert your name, your family's names, your workplace, your church, and your community.

These are not just words; they are weapons in the hands of the faithful.

And remember this promise: "The prayer of a righteous person is powerful and effective."— James 5:16 (NIV)

PART ONE

PRAYERS FOR HOME AND FAMILY

Prayer for Peace in the Home

Heavenly Father,

I lift up my home before You today. Lord, You see every corner, every room, and every heart that walks through these doors. I ask You to flood this house with Your peace that surpasses all understanding. Where there has been shouting, let there be gentleness. Where there has been the silence of hurt, let there be healing words. Where there has been chaos, bring Your order.

Father, I declare that this home belongs to You. I invite Your Spirit to dwell richly within these walls. Drive out every spirit of strife, anger, and bitterness. Replace them with laughter, joy, and the warmth of unconditional love. May this place be a safe haven, a place of rest and renewal, not conflict or unrest.

Lord, teach my family and me to speak life into one another. Remind us daily that love covers a multitude of sins. May forgiveness flow quickly, and may patience rise in us like a shield. When we feel overwhelmed, bring us back to Your Word and to Your presence.

I declare that no weapon formed against this home shall prosper. As for me and my house, we will serve the Lord. Father, let Your angels stand guard at our doors, protecting us from harm and keeping peace within. Thank You for hearing this urgent prayer.

In the name of Jesus Christ of Nazareth, Amen.

Prayer for a Troubled Marriage

Lord God,

You see the cracks in my marriage, the words left unsaid and the wounds too deep for human hands to heal. Father, I place this marriage into Your hands. You are the Restorer of broken covenants and the Mender of what seems shattered beyond repair.

Give us soft hearts once again. Where bitterness has grown, pull it up by the roots and plant forgiveness instead. Teach us to listen, not just to respond, but to truly hear one another. Heal every place where trust has been broken, and let honesty become the foundation we build upon.

Help me to love as You love, without conditions and without keeping records of wrongs. When anger rises, let Your Spirit remind me of patience. When silence stretches too long, let Your whisper break it with tenderness. Where there is distance, draw us close. Where there is pride, humble us with Your grace.

Lord, I refuse to let the enemy steal what You have blessed. I speak life into this marriage today. I call forth unity, restoration, and love. May this marriage not only survive but thrive, becoming a testimony of Your power to restore.

Do what only You can do. In the name of Jesus Christ of Nazareth, Amen.

Prayer for Parenting Wisdom

Gracious Father,

Parenting is not easy, and today I come before You feeling the weight of responsibility. You have entrusted me with precious lives, and I confess that I do not always know what to do. But You are the perfect Father, and I look to You for guidance.

Fill me with wisdom beyond my experience, patience beyond my natural ability, and insight that comes only from You. Help me discipline with love, not frustration. Teach me to encourage rather than tear down. Let my words be seeds of life that grow strong, godly character in my children.

When I feel tired and at my breaking point, remind me that Your strength is made perfect in my weakness. Quiet my worries with Your peace. When doubt creeps in, remind me that You chose me for this role and that You will equip me.

Cover my children with protection, discernment, and courage to stand for what is right. Shape their hearts to love what is good and to walk in Your ways, even when it is difficult. I surrender my parenting to You. I cannot do this without You. In the name of Jesus Christ of Nazareth, Amen.

Prayer for a Rebellious Teen

Lord,

You see my child, and You know the battles raging in their heart. I bring my son or daughter before You, knowing that only You can truly reach them.

Silence every lie that says rebellion is freedom. Show them that true freedom is found in You alone. I speak life over their destiny and declare that they will not be lost to destructive choices or harmful influences.

Give me patience when I feel weary and strength when my heart feels heavy. Teach me to love consistently, pray faithfully, and believe even when the situation feels impossible. Help me see my child through Your eyes, not defined by mistakes, but by purpose.

Surround them with godly mentors, friends, and influences. Break every chain of rebellion and replace it with humility, peace, and obedience. Restore joy and tenderness to their heart. Their story is not over. In the name of Jesus Christ of Nazareth, Amen.

Prayer for Family Unity

Heavenly Father,
You created families to reflect Your love, yet division has found its way into mine. Lord, I ask You to heal every fracture. Where there has been jealousy, bring celebration. Where there has been hurt, bring forgiveness. Where there has been silence, open the door to reconciliation.

Teach us to speak kindly, listen patiently, and forgive quickly. Remove every spirit of division and replace it with the bond of peace. Unite us by Your Spirit so that our home may once again be filled with joy, laughter, and unconditional love.

Help us stand together, not against one another. Let us be quick to pray for each other, defend one another, and encourage one another. What You have joined together, let nothing divide. In the name of Jesus Christ of Nazareth, Amen.

Prayer for Financial Provision in the Household

Father,

You see every need in this home, the bills, the responsibilities, and the concerns that weigh on my heart. I ask You to provide for this household according to Your riches and faithfulness.

Remove fear and replace it with trust. Give me wisdom to manage what You provide, discipline to steward it well, and creativity to seek new opportunities. Open doors of provision and unexpected blessing.

Let this home lack nothing it truly needs. May there be enough not only to sustain us, but also to bless others. I declare this home blessed, not burdened. In the name of Jesus Christ of Nazareth, Amen.

Prayer for Protection Over Loved Ones

Lord,

I place my family under Your protection today. I ask You to surround them wherever they go, at work, at school, on the road, and at rest. Protect us from accidents, sickness, violence, and unseen danger. Strengthen our faith so fear does not take root in our hearts. You are our refuge and our fortress.

I declare that my family will live and walk in Your covering and care. In the name of Jesus Christ of Nazareth, Amen.

Prayer for Restoration of Broken Relationships

Scripture: "Bear with each other and forgive one another if any of you has a grievance against someone. Forgive as the Lord forgave you." — Colossians 3:13 (NIV)

Merciful Father,
You see the brokenness in my family. I bring before You every strained and damaged relationship. Heal what has been torn apart. Remove pride and stubbornness. Teach us humility, compassion, and forgiveness. Let healing begin with me. Show me how to extend grace even when it is difficult.

Restore closeness where there has been distance and love where there has been indifference. I trust You to bring beauty from ashes. In the name of Jesus Christ of Nazareth, Amen.

Prayer for Peaceful Sleep & Safety at Night

Heavenly Father,

As night falls, I place this household in Your care. Drive away every spirit of fear, anxiety, and restlessness. Replace them with peace and rest.

Let every heart sleep safely, and every mind rest without worry. Station Your angels around this home and guard us through the night.

Thank You for being our protector who never sleeps nor slumbers. In the name of Jesus Christ of Nazareth, Amen.

Prayer for Love and Patience in Daily Family Life

Gracious Lord,

Family life is a gift, yet it comes with challenges. I ask You to fill this home with love and patience. Teach us to respond with kindness and grace rather than frustration.

When misunderstandings arise, let forgiveness flow quickly. Help us choose love daily and put one another before ourselves.
Let our home be known for encouragement, laughter, and peace. Thank You for the gift of family and for walking with us through every season.
In the name of Jesus Christ of Nazareth, Amen.

PART TWO

WORK & CAREER

Prayer for Career Guidance

Heavenly Father,

You know the path before me, and You see what I cannot. Lord, I bring my career into Your hands. Sometimes I feel lost, unsure which direction to take, but You are my Shepherd, and You promised to lead me beside still waters and guide me into righteousness.

"Trust in the Lord with all your heart and lean not on your own understanding; in all your ways submit to Him, and He will make your paths straight." (Proverbs 3:5–6)

Father, close doors that are not from You and open the doors that align with Your will. Remove every distraction, every opportunity that looks good but is not God-ordained. Teach me to trust Your timing, not rush ahead of You, and not lag behind.

I surrender my ambitions to You. Take my gifts, my skills, my education, and my experiences, and use them for Your glory. Lord, plant me where I will flourish, not just to make money, but to make a difference.

I believe You have a plan for me, a hope and a future. Let me walk confidently in that plan, trusting that You will order my steps.

In the name of Jesus Christ of Nazareth, Amen.

Prayer for Workplace Peace

Prince of Peace,
You see the tensions, the politics, the misunderstandings, and the stress in my workplace. Lord, I ask You to breathe peace into that atmosphere. Let Your Spirit rule where confusion and division try to reign.

"Blessed are the peacemakers, for they will be called children of God." (Matthew 5:9)
Father, protect me from toxic words and negative attitudes. Give me grace to respond with kindness even when others are harsh. Let me be a light in that place, carrying Your peace wherever I go.
Help me not only to work hard but also to love well. Remind me that every co-worker, even the difficult ones, is someone You love. Change me where I need changing, and soften the hearts of those around me.

Let my workplace become a place where peace flows, teamwork thrives, and respect is practiced. May Your presence follow me into every meeting, every conversation, and every task. In the name of Jesus Christ of Nazareth, Amen.

Prayer for Strength Against Stress

Father God,

Sometimes the workload feels overwhelming, the deadlines impossible, and the expectations too heavy. Lord, I cast every burden at Your feet right now. You said, "Come to Me all who are weary and heavy laden, and I will give you rest."

"I can do all things through Christ who strengthens me." (Philippians 4:13)

Fill me with supernatural strength. Help me work with focus, efficiency, and clarity of mind. Calm the racing thoughts that make me anxious. Replace them with Your peace and steady my heart.

Lord, remind me that my worth is not found in how much I accomplish, but in who I am in You. Give me wisdom to prioritize, courage to say no when needed, and rest when my body is weary. When stress tries to steal my joy, help me cling to You, my source of strength. In the name of Jesus Christ of Nazareth, Amen.

Prayer for Promotion & Favor

Lord of Favor,

I place my career before You and ask for Your divine hand to open doors that no one can shut. I believe You are the One who lifts up and promotes. "For promotion comes neither from the east, nor from the west, nor from the south. But God is the Judge: He puts down one, and sets up another." (Psalm 75:6–7)

If promotion is in Your will, let it come in Your timing. Let my work speak for itself, and let my integrity shine brighter than competition. Place my name on the hearts of decision-makers, and let favor surround me like a shield.

But even as I ask, I surrender. If this is not my season, give me patience. If this is my time, give me humility to carry success wisely. Let my promotion glorify You and give me greater influence to serve with excellence.

In the name of Jesus Christ of Nazareth, Amen.

Prayer for Integrity at Work

Holy God,

In a world where shortcuts, dishonesty, and compromise seem normal, help me stand firm in integrity. Let my yes be yes and my no be no.

"The integrity of the upright guides them, but the unfaithful are destroyed by their duplicity." (Proverbs 11:3)

When I am tempted to cut corners, remind me that I work for You first, not just for people. When I am pressured to compromise, give me boldness to stand in truth.

Help me be trustworthy, dependable, and honest in all things. Let others see Your character in me, even in the smallest details. In the name of Jesus Christ of Nazareth, Amen.

A Prayer for Business Owners

Lord of wisdom and provision,
I lift up every business I own, manage, or dream of starting. You are the Author of vision and the Giver of every good idea.
Grant me clarity of mind and purity of motive. Fill me with wisdom to lead with integrity, courage to take bold yet righteous steps, and patience to wait on Your perfect timing.

The bible says, "Commit to the Lord whatever you do, and He will establish your plans." (Proverbs 16:3)

Bless every client, employee, and customer connected to this business. Let every transaction be rooted in honesty, every service in excellence, and every interaction in kindness.

Protect this work from theft, fraud, deceit, and every attack meant to destroy what You have built. Teach me to be a faithful steward of all You entrust to me.
In the name of Jesus Christ of Nazareth, Amen.

Prayer for Protection from Unfair Treatment

Father,

You are the God of justice, and You see every injustice in my workplace. Protect me from false accusations, unfair treatment, discrimination, and hidden agendas.

Father your words says, "No weapon formed against me shall prosper, and every tongue which rises against me in judgment You shall condemn." (Isaiah 54:17)

When I am overlooked, remind me that You see me. When I am treated unfairly, help me respond with grace, not bitterness. Vindicate me by Your hand, not mine.

Guard my heart from resentment, and keep my character upright even in trial.

In the name of Jesus Christ of Nazareth, Amen.

Prayer for Creativity and Innovation

"I have filled him with the Spirit of God, with wisdom, with understanding, with knowledge, and with all kinds of skills." (Exodus 31:3)

Creator God,

You designed the heavens with detail and beauty, and You placed creativity within me. Awaken my mind with fresh ideas, innovative solutions, and creative strategies for my work.

Remove mental blocks and fear of failure. Let boldness rise in me to try new things and step into new territory.

May every idea be aligned with Your wisdom and timing.
In the name of Jesus Christ of Nazareth, Amen.

Prayer for Balance Between Work & Family

Father,

You know how easily work can consume my time and attention. Teach me balance. Help me work diligently without neglecting those I love.

"What good will it be for someone to gain the whole world, yet forfeit their soul?" (Matthew 16:26)

Give me wisdom to know when to close the laptop, silence the phone, and give my full presence to my family. Let my work bless my home, not steal me from it. In the name of Jesus Christ of Nazareth, Amen.

Prayer for Joy in Daily Tasks

Whatever you do, work at it with all your heart, as working for the Lord, not for human masters." (Colossians 3:23)

Gracious Lord,
Sometimes work feels mundane and heavy. Restore joy in my daily tasks. Help me see purpose in the ordinary.
"Whatever you do, work at it with all your heart, as working for the Lord, not for human masters." (Colossians 3:23)

Let my attitude shift from frustration to gratitude. Let my work become worship and let joy overflow even in small responsibilities. In the name of Jesus Christ of Nazareth, Amen.

PART THREE

SINGLE PARENTS

Prayer for Single Mothers' Strength

Lord,

It is just me here, raising my child or children, and some days the weight feels too heavy. There are moments when I feel like I cannot go on, but I know I am not alone. You promised to be a husband to the widow and a Father to the fatherless. You see me, and You see my children. "He gives strength to the weary and increases the power of the weak." (Isaiah 40:29)

Strengthen me, Father. When I feel weary, lift me up. When I cry silently at night, remind me that You bottle every tear. Give me courage to keep moving forward even when I feel like giving up.
I pray that my children will not feel less because there is only one parent in the home. Fill every gap with Your love. Cover our family with Your presence. Let my children see resilience, faith, and unconditional love in me.

I trust You to be what I cannot be, to supply what I cannot provide, and to strengthen me when I feel weak.
In the name of Jesus Christ of Nazareth, Amen.

Prayer for Single Fathers' Guidance

Heavenly Father,
Sometimes I feel the pressure of being both father and mother. I try to guide, provide, and protect all at once, and I confess that I do not always know what I am doing. But You are my Father, and I lean on You for wisdom.
"If any of you lacks wisdom, you should ask God, who gives generously to all without finding fault, and it will be given to you." (James 1:5)

Show me how to raise my children with patience, discipline, and love. Help me to be present in their lives, even when work and responsibilities pull me away. Give me courage to talk about feelings, to listen deeply, and to lead with gentleness.

Provide for this household. Give me the ability to put food on the table and hope in their hearts. Teach me to model integrity and faith so my children will know what a godly man looks like.
I surrender my pride and ask You to fill the places where I fall short. In the name of Jesus Christ of Nazareth, Amen.

Prayer for Provision for Children

Lord,
There are moments when I do not know how I will stretch what little I have to cover everything. You see the bills, the shoes my child has outgrown, the lunch money, and the school supplies. Father, I need Your provision.

"And my God will meet all your needs according to the riches of His glory in Christ Jesus." (Philippians 4:19)
Open doors of opportunity. Provide steady income. Let unexpected blessings find their way to us. Help me manage wisely what You place in my hands.

More than money, I ask for joy in this home. Let my children never feel the weight of lack, but instead feel surrounded by love. Remind them that You are their ultimate Provider.
Thank You for meeting every need, even in ways I do not always see. In the name of Jesus Christ of Nazareth, Amen.

Prayer for the Protection of Single-Parent Homes

Father,

As a single parent, I sometimes feel vulnerable, like everything depends on me. But You are our Protector. I place this home under Your covering.

"For He will command His angels concerning you to guard you in all your ways." (Psalm 91:11)

Send Your angels to stand guard around our house, our beds, and our lives. Keep us safe from violence, sickness, and harm. Let this home be a place of peace, refuge, and safety.

Calm my fears when they rise. Remind me that You neither slumber nor sleep. In the name of Jesus Christ of Nazareth, Amen.

Prayer for Peace in Lonely Nights

Lord,

When the children are asleep and the house is quiet, loneliness creeps in. Sometimes I ache for companionship, for someone to share the weight of this journey with. You see my heart.

"I will never leave you nor forsake you." (Deuteronomy 31:6)

Be my companion in the silence. Hold me in the emptiness. Fill the quiet spaces of my soul with Your presence and peace.

If it is Your will for me to have someone in the future, I trust You with the timing. Until then, strengthen me in You. Remind me that my joy comes from You alone. In the name of Jesus Christ of Nazareth, Amen.

Prayer for Wisdom in Raising Sons

Heavenly Father,

I desire to raise my son to be strong, kind, and Godly. As a single parent, I sometimes feel unqualified, but I trust You to fill the gaps. "Train up a child in the way he should go, and when he is old he will not depart from it." (Proverbs 22:6)

Send Godly role models, mentors, and leaders into his life. Protect him from destructive influences. Give me wisdom to discipline with love and to speak words that shape his character.

Let him grow into a man who honors You, respects others, and walks in integrity. In the name of Jesus Christ of Nazareth, Amen.

Prayer for Patience in Raising Daughters

Gracious Lord,

My daughter is growing, and with her growth come challenges, emotions, questions, and identity struggles. Lord, I want to guide her well, but sometimes I lose my patience. Forgive me, Father.

Your Word says in Colossians 3:21, "Fathers, do not embitter your children, or they will become discouraged."

Teach me how to listen without judgment, to correct without crushing, and to encourage without smothering. Help me to model womanhood in a way that points her to You. Let her see in me strength, dignity, and faith.

Protect her from lies that say she isn't enough. Fill her heart with confidence, self-worth, and purity. Lord, may she see herself through Your eyes, precious, chosen, and loved.

Give me patience for the hard days and joy for the sweet ones. Thank You for the gift of my daughter. In Jesus' name, Amen.

Prayer for Endurance in Financial Struggles

Father God,

There are days when I feel exhausted from juggling bills, stretching groceries, and making ends meet. Lord, I confess, I get tired of struggling. But I also know You are my strength. Your Word says in Galatians 6:9, "Let us not become weary in doing good, for at the proper time we will reap a harvest if we do not give up."

Give me endurance, Father. Help me press on even when it feels like too much. Provide for this family in ways that remind me You are still with us. Teach me to be grateful for what we have, even when it seems small.

Father, don't let my children feel the weight of my worry. Let them see hope in me, not despair. And Lord, surprise us with Your provision, so that we may testify of Your goodness. In Jesus' name, Amen.

Prayer for Confidence and Self-Worth

Lord,

As a single parent, sometimes I feel like I've failed. Society whispers that I'm not enough, that my family is broken. But Father, I reject those lies. My worth is not defined by my marital status, but by Your love for me. Your Word says in Psalm 139:14, "I praise you because I am fearfully and wonderfully made; your works are wonderful, I know that full well."

Remind me that I am chosen, loved, and called. Remind me that I am strong, capable, and enough, because You are with me. Help me to walk with my head high, not in shame.

Lord, let my children see confidence in me, so they too may grow secure in who they are. Teach me to silence the voices of doubt and to rest in the truth of Your word.
I am not less than. I am Your child, and that is enough. In Jesus' name, Amen.

Prayer for Godly Role Models for Children

Heavenly Father,
I know I cannot do this alone. My children need influences beyond me, people who will encourage, guide, and model Your ways. Lord, bring Godly teachers, mentors, pastors, and friends into their lives who will speak truth with love and walk in humility before You.

Your Word says in Proverbs 13:20, "Walk with the wise and become wise, for a companion of fools suffers harm." So I ask, Father, that You surround them with wisdom. Let them walk with those who know and love You deeply. Place people in their paths who will help them discern right from wrong, truth from lies, and love from selfishness.

Remove negative influences that would draw their hearts away from You. Shield them from destructive friendships, harmful habits, and voices that seek to distort their identity or purpose. Instead, plant them in communities where they will be nurtured, loved, and supported, where Your Spirit is alive and Your Word is honored.

Father, when I fall short, be the father and mother they need. When I am silent, be the voice that whispers wisdom in their ears. When I am not near, let them feel Your nearness. May they grow to know that You are their truest Friend, their ultimate Counselor, and their constant help.
Let Your Holy Spirit teach them in every season, how to choose kindness over anger, forgiveness over bitterness, courage over fear, and faith over doubt. Build in them hearts that long to serve, to give, and to love as You love.

I thank You in advance, Lord, for every Godly influence You will send, the teachers who will inspire them, the friends who will strengthen their faith, the mentors who will challenge them to grow, and the church family that will remind them who they are in You.

Keep their hearts soft, their minds sharp, and their spirits anchored in truth. Let their lives bring You glory in every word, every choice, and every relationship.

In Jesus' precious name, Amen.

PART FOUR

CHILDREN & YOUTH

Prayer for a Young Daughter's Self-Worth

Father God,
I see my little girl growing up in a world that tries to tell her she's not enough. Lord, I pray that her worth will not come from the mirror, from social media, or from the opinions of others, but from You.

Your Word says in Psalm 139:14, "I praise you because I am fearfully and wonderfully made; your works are wonderful, I know that full well."
Father, let her know she is fearfully and wonderfully made. Protect her from lies that say she has to look a certain way to be beautiful. Help me, Lord, to speak life over her every single day, reminding her that she is chosen, loved, and precious in Your sight.

When insecurity tries to creep in, let Your truth rise in her spirit. Surround her with friends who lift her up, not tear her down. And Lord, give me the wisdom to model confidence and joy so she sees it lived out.
I declare she will walk boldly, knowing she is a daughter of the King. In Jesus' name, Amen.

Prayer for a Son's Future

Lord,

As I watch my son grow, my heart is both proud and anxious. I think about the man he will become, and I place his future in Your hands.

Your Word says in Jeremiah 29:11, "For I know the plans I have for you," declares the Lord, "plans to prosper you and not to harm you, plans to give you hope and a future."

Father, guide his steps. Protect him from wrong paths and lead him into purpose. Give him a heart of courage, a spirit of humility, and a mind filled with wisdom. Let him rise into manhood with integrity and strength.

Keep him from influences that would destroy him. Shield him from addiction, from violence, from destructive choices. Instead, surround him with mentors, role models, and friends who push him toward greatness.

Lord, let him become the man You created him to be faithful, kind, and strong in You. His future is secure because it rests in Your hands. In Jesus' name, Amen.

Prayer for Protection at School

Father,

When I drop my child off at school, my heart sometimes feels heavy. The world can be dangerous, and I can't always be there to protect them. But Lord, You can.

Your Word says in Psalm 121:7-8, "The Lord will keep you from all harm, he will watch over your life; the Lord will watch over your coming and going both now and forevermore."

Cover them as they walk the hallways, as they sit in class, and as they play outside. Guard them from bullies, from violence, from harmful influences. Give them favor with teachers and kindness with friends.

Lord, sharpen their minds for learning, but more importantly, protect their hearts. Let no fear take root. Remind them that You are with them, even when I am not.

I place them in Your care today, Father, knowing that no one protects better than You. In Jesus' name, Amen.

Prayer Against Peer Pressure

Lord,

I know how strong the pull of peers can be, especially for my child who just wants to fit in. Father, I ask You to give them strength to stand firm, even when it's hard.

Your Word says in Romans 12:2, "Do not conform to the pattern of this world, but be transformed by the renewing of your mind. Then you will be able to test and approve what God's will is, his good, pleasing and perfect will."

Help them say no when they need to, even if it means standing alone. Remind them that being accepted by You is greater than being accepted by the crowd. Place a deep conviction in their heart to choose what is right, not just what is popular.

Lord, bring the right friends into their life, those who will encourage them to walk in truth. Protect them from relationships that would lead them astray. And Father, give me wisdom to speak into their life with love, not condemnation.

I declare my child will not be swallowed by peer pressure but will rise as a leader, not a follower. In Jesus' name, Amen.

Prayer for Academic Excellence

Father God,

I pray over my child's education today. Sometimes school feels overwhelming, and the pressure to succeed is heavy. But Lord, You gave my child a mind capable of learning, growing, and excelling.

Your Word says in Daniel 1:17, "To these four young men God gave knowledge and understanding of all kinds of literature and learning. And Daniel could understand visions and dreams of all kinds."

Bless their memory, sharpen their focus, and give them clarity in understanding. When they struggle, remind them not to give up but to lean on You for strength.

Lord, remove distractions that steal their time. Give them confidence when tests come and peace when they feel anxious. Let learning be a joy, not a burden.

Father, I declare that my child will excel, not for pride's sake, but to glorify You with the gifts You've given them. Thank You for filling their mind with wisdom and creativity. In Jesus' name, Amen.

Prayer for Godly Friendships

Lord,
I know how powerful friendships are in shaping my child's future. Father, I ask You to send godly friends into their life, friends who will lift them up, not drag them down.

Your Word says in 1 Corinthians 15:33, "Do not be misled: 'Bad company corrupts good character.'"
Remove toxic relationships, no matter how hard it may feel. Protect my child from those who would influence them toward destruction. Surround them with people who speak encouragement, who share their faith, and who challenge them to grow.

Father, let my child also be a good friend, kind, loyal, forgiving, and trustworthy. Let their circle of influence reflect Your love.
Thank You, Lord, for handpicking friends who will walk alongside them in this journey. In Jesus' name, Amen.

Prayer Against Childhood Abuse

Father,

My heart trembles at the thought of harm coming to my child. Lord, I ask You to shield them from every form of abuse, physical, emotional, or spiritual.

Your Word says in Psalm 91:4, "He will cover you with his feathers, and under his wings you will find refuge; his faithfulness will be your shield and rampart."

Keep predators far from them. Expose every hidden danger and every wrong intention. Surround my child with safe adults, safe places, and safe relationships.

Father, if my child has already experienced pain, I ask for Your healing touch. Restore innocence where it was stolen. Replace fear with peace, shame with dignity, and brokenness with wholeness.

Lord, I declare that no weapon formed against my child will prosper. Cover them with Your mighty hand and let their childhood be filled with joy, love, and safety. In Jesus' name, Amen.

Prayer for Mental and Emotional Healing

Lord,

I see the heaviness sometimes in my child's eyes, the sadness, the anxiety, the weight they can't put into words. Father, I bring their heart to You. Your Word says in Psalm 34:18, "The Lord is close to the brokenhearted and saves those who are crushed in spirit."

Heal them emotionally, mentally, and spiritually. Take away the fear that haunts them, the sadness that lingers, and the anxiety that steals their joy. Replace it with peace, laughter, and hope.

Father, let my child know they are never alone. Teach me how to listen better, to love more deeply, and to provide the support they need. Surround them with counselors, teachers, and friends who will speak life into them.

I declare my child will walk in freedom and joy. Thank You for being the Healer of hearts. In Jesus' name, Amen.

Prayer for Creative Talents to Shine

Father,

I see the gifts You've placed in my child, the way they sing, draw, build, or create. Lord, I pray those gifts will not be hidden but nurtured.

Your Word says in 1 Peter 4:10, "Each of you should use whatever gift you have received to serve others, as faithful stewards of God's grace in its various forms."

Open doors for them to explore their talents. Give them courage to express themselves, even when they fear judgment. Remind them that every creative spark is a reflection of Your image.

Father, protect their creativity from comparison and discouragement. Let it flourish into something beautiful that glorifies You. Use their talents to bless others and bring joy to their lives.

Thank You for making my child wonderfully unique. In Jesus' name, Amen.

Prayer for Respect Toward Parents

Lord,

Parenting can be hard, especially when children test boundaries. Father, I ask that You place in my child a heart of honor and respect.

Your Word says in Ephesians 6:1–2, "Children, obey your parents in the Lord, for this is right. 'Honor your father and mother' which is the first commandment with a promise."

Help them to see that my correction comes from love. Teach them to value obedience, not as punishment, but as protection. Let them grow into adults who honor authority, beginning with their parents.

Father, help me to model respect too through my words, my patience, and my actions. Let our relationship be built on mutual love and trust.

I declare that disrespect will not take root in this home. Instead, love, honor, and peace will guide our family. In Jesus' name, Amen.

PART FIVE

EXTENDED FAMILY

Prayer for a Loving Uncle

Father God,

Thank You for blessing me with my uncle. He has been more than just a relative; he's been a mentor, a supporter, and at times, even a father figure. Lord, I lift him up to You today.

Your Word says in Proverbs 17:17, "A friend loves at all times, and a brother is born for a time of adversity."

Strengthen him in his health, his work, and his relationships. If he carries burdens he doesn't talk about, lighten his load. Remind him that he is valued and loved.

Father, I pray our relationship grows stronger. Help me to honor him with words of gratitude and acts of kindness. If there has ever been hurt between us, Lord, heal it. Restore laughter, trust, and closeness.

Bless his household, his finances, and his dreams. May his life continue to be a blessing to mine and to everyone around him. Thank You, Lord, for the gift of my uncle. In Jesus' name, Amen.

Prayer for a Caring Aunt

Lord,

I lift up my aunt before You today. She has been a safe place; someone I could talk to when no one else would listen. Father, bless her for the love she pours into our family.

Your Word says in Proverbs 31:26, "She speaks with wisdom, and faithful instruction is on her tongue."

Give her peace in her mind, joy in her heart, and strength in her body. If she feels overlooked or unappreciated, remind her that You see her sacrifices.

Lord, let me also give back to her. Help me to honor her, support her, and be present for her the way she has been present for me. Restore her when she feels weary and surround her with love when she feels alone.

Thank You, Father, for my aunt's caring heart. Let her continue to be a light in our family. In Jesus' name, Amen.

Prayer for Grandparents' Health

Father,

I thank You for the gift of my grandparents. They are pillars of wisdom, strength, and love in this family. Lord, I pray over their health today.

Your Word says in Isaiah 46:4, "Even to your old age and gray hairs I am he, I am he who will sustain you. I have made you and I will carry you; I will sustain you and I will rescue you."

Strengthen their bodies, renew their energy, and comfort them in their old age. Where there is pain, bring relief. Where there is loneliness, bring companionship. Where there is weariness, bring peace.

Father, bless them with joy in their remaining years. Let them see their legacy of love passed down through their children and grandchildren. Remind me to cherish them while I still have them, to listen to their stories, and to honor them with my time.

Thank You, Lord, for the heritage of faith and love they've given us. Keep them in Your care until their last breath. In Jesus' name, Amen.

Prayer for Cousins' Unity

Lord,

Thank You for the beautiful gift of family and for the cousins You've placed in my life. We share roots, memories, and laughter that tie our hearts together. Sometimes we're close, and sometimes distance or life's busyness pulls us apart, but I know that Your love can keep us connected no matter where we are.

Your Word reminds us, "How good and pleasant it is when God's people live together in unity!" (Psalm 133:1) Father, I ask You to bless our relationship with that kind of unity, strong, peaceful, and full of love. Remove anything that divides us, jealousy, pride, competition, or misunderstandings, and replace them with patience, humility, and kindness.

Help us to cherish one another, to be quick to forgive, and slow to take offense. Let laughter and encouragement flow freely between us. Teach us to celebrate each other's victories and to stand together in times of struggle.

Lord, may our bond not just be through blood, but through genuine love and faith. Let our unity be a reflection of Your heart, a testimony of grace and goodness that others can see.

Thank You for every memory we share and for all the moments still to come. Keep our connection strong, our hearts tender, and our love unwavering. In Jesus' name, Amen.

Prayer for Siblings in Conflict

Father God,

You see the tension between me and my sibling. Lord, it hurts that the one who should be closest feels so far away. I don't want bitterness to take root.

Your Word says in Ephesians 4:32, "Be kind and compassionate to one another, forgiving each other, just as in Christ God forgave you."
Father, soften both our hearts. Heal old wounds and replace anger with forgiveness. Remind us of the bond we share, that we grew up under the same roof, shared the same love, and are connected for life.

Teach us to talk without shouting, to listen without judging, and to forgive without keeping score. Lord, let reconciliation begin with me. Give me the humility to reach out, and give my sibling the grace to respond.

Father, restore our relationship. I refuse to let division win. In Jesus' name, Amen.

Prayer for Estranged Relatives

Dear Lord,

My heart aches for the family members I no longer speak to. Somewhere along the way, distance, pride, and pain built walls between us. What once felt close now feels cold, and it grieves me deeply. Father, You see every wound, every misunderstanding, and every unspoken word. I ask You to heal what feels broken beyond repair.

Your Word says in 2 Corinthians 5:18, "All this is from God, who reconciled us to himself through Christ and gave us the ministry of reconciliation." Lord, I ask You to breathe that same spirit of reconciliation into my family. Where there has been silence, bring gentle conversation. Where there has been bitterness, sow seeds of forgiveness. Melt hardened hearts, including my own. Help me to release any offense I've carried, even the ones I justified. Teach us to see each other through Your eyes, with compassion instead of judgment, and with mercy instead of pride.

Father, restore what the enemy tried to destroy. Repair broken trust, renew lost affection, and bring beauty from the ashes of our past. Even if reconciliation takes time, let healing begin today, first in our hearts, then in our words, and finally in our actions.

Thank You, Lord, for being the God who restores. I place every strained relationship into Your hands and trust You to bring peace in Your perfect way and timing.
In Jesus' name, Amen.

Prayer for In-Laws Peace

Father God,

I bring my in-laws before You today with a humble heart. Family relationships can be both a blessing and a challenge, and sometimes it's not easy to find harmony. But Lord, You are the Elohim of peace, and I know You can bring understanding where there has been strain and unity where there has been division.

Your Word says in Romans 12:18, "If it is possible, as far as it depends on you, live at peace with everyone." Father, I take that to heart. Help me to do my part to walk in peace, even when it feels difficult. Where there has been misunderstanding, bring clarity and open communication. Where there has been criticism, let compassion soften our words. Where there has been tension, pour out patience, humility, and grace.

Father, bless my in-laws with health, joy, and favor. Let our relationship be marked by mutual respect, laughter, and support. May we learn to appreciate one another's differences and celebrate the gift of being joined together through love and family.

Thank You, Lord, for weaving them into my life and using every interaction, good or hard, to shape me into someone more patient, kind, and Christlike. May Your peace reign in our hearts and our homes, in Jesus' name, Amen.

Prayer for Family Gatherings

Lord,

Family gatherings can be both joyful and stressful. Sometimes they bring laughter, and sometimes they bring conflict. Father, I ask You to cover our gatherings with peace and love.

Your Word says in Colossians 3:14, "And over all these virtues put on love, which binds them all together in perfect unity." Help us to clothe ourselves with patience, kindness, and humility, so that love will lead every word and action.

Let our conversations be filled with encouragement, not criticism. Let our time together be marked by laughter, not arguments. Protect us from misunderstandings, jealousy, or division. When differences arise, remind us that grace is stronger than pride. Teach us to listen more than we speak and to forgive faster than we take offense. May Your Spirit guide every moment so that peace remains in our midst.

Lord, bless each person who gathers, those near and those far away. Let joy fill our hearts and gratitude fill our words. Keep us mindful that family is a precious gift, not to be taken for granted.

Father, bless the food, the fellowship, and the memories we make. Let our time together remind us of the blessing of family. May our gatherings reflect Your love and unity.
In Jesus' name, Amen.

Prayer for Family Heritage & Blessings

Father in heaven,
I thank You for the heritage of family. The traditions, the culture, the faith, it all matters. Lord, I pray that the blessings of past generations will flow down into this one. Your Word says in Psalm 103:17, "But from everlasting to everlasting the Lord's love is with those who fear him, and his righteousness with their children's children." Thank You for being faithful through every generation, guiding our family through seasons of joy and challenge.

Break every generational curse and replace it with generational blessings. Let faith, kindness, strength, and love be what we pass on. May my children and their children walk in the legacy of godliness and grace.

Remind us, Lord, that the choices we make today shape the generations to come. Help us to sow seeds of grace and wisdom that will produce lasting fruit in our family line. May our home be known for peace, prayer, and love that reflects Your heart.

Lord, remind me to honor the good in my family heritage and to let go of what does not reflect You. Thank You for writing a story of redemption and blessing over us. I declare that my family line is covered, favored, and blessed by Your hand. In Jesus' name, Amen.

Prayer for Generational Healing

Heavenly Father,

I see patterns in my family, addiction, anger, broken marriages, and poverty. Lord, I ask You to break these cycles in Jesus' name. What has wounded generations before me will not continue through me. Your Word says in 2 Corinthians 5:17, "Therefore, if anyone is in Christ, the new creation has come: The old has gone, the new is here!" I hold onto this promise, believing that through Your power, a new story begins in my family today.

Replace anger with peace, addiction with freedom, brokenness with restoration, and poverty with abundance. Let Your mercy uproot every curse and plant seeds of blessing that will bear fruit for generations to come.

Father, let me be the one who changes the story for my children and grandchildren. Start the healing with me. Give me wisdom to live differently, courage to forgive, and faith to trust Your timing. Let Your Spirit flow through our family tree, healing roots and branches alike.

Thank You, Lord, that we don't have to repeat the past. In You, we are made new. May our family forever be marked by Your redemption, peace, and love. In Jesus' name, Amen.

PART SIX

EMOTIONAL STRUGGLES

Prayer Against Anger

"Be angry, and do not sin; do not let the sun go down on your anger." –
Ephesians 4:26

Dear Lord,

I confess I've been carrying anger in my heart. Sometimes it rises so quickly I can hardly control it. Words spill out that I wish I could take back. Father, I don't want this anger to destroy my relationships or steal my peace.

Help me, Lord. Calm the storm inside me. Teach me to pause, to breathe, and to listen before I speak. Replace the fire of rage with the fire of Your Spirit, gentle, patient, and kind.

When old wounds try to reopen and bitterness resurfaces, remind me of Your mercy. Just as You forgive me daily, help me to extend that same forgiveness to others.

Holy Spirit, fill every space in me where anger once lived.

Let Your presence wash over my heart like a healing river. Break every chain of resentment, every pattern of harshness, and every lie that fuels my temper. Speak peace where there has been pain. Let Your love consume every part of me until anger no longer has power or place.

Father, let love and patience rise higher than my anger. Fill me with peace that passes all understanding. I surrender this temper to You. Heal the root of my pain, and let me walk in gentleness, grace, and strength.

In Jesus' name, Amen.

Prayer Against Depression

"The Lord is near to the brokenhearted and saves the crushed in spirit."
– Psalm 34:18

Father God,
Some days it feels like a heavy blanket is over me, darkness I can't shake. I smile on the outside, but inside I feel empty. Lord, You see me when no one else does.

Lift this weight from me. Break through the clouds of sadness with the light of Your love. Restore joy to my soul. Help me believe again that life is worth living. When I feel like I'm sinking, remind me that You are near. Wrap me in Your comfort and whisper hope into my weary heart. Send people who will encourage me, not judge me.

Father, replace my despair with divine strength.
When I can't find words to pray, let my tears speak to You. When I can't stand, carry me. Remind me that healing may take time, but with You, it is certain.

Holy Spirit, fill my heart with light again.
Push back every shadow of hopelessness with the power of Your presence. Let joy rise within me, not based on circumstances, but on Your unchanging love. Let today mark the beginning of my restoration.

Father, I refuse to let depression define me. My identity is not in despair but in being Your child. Thank You for holding me when I can't hold myself. In Jesus' name, Amen.

Prayer Against Anxiety

"Cast all your anxiety on Him because He cares for you."
1 Peter 5:7

Abba Father in Heaven,
My thoughts race, my chest feels tight, and worry keeps me awake at night. Father, You see how anxiety grips me. I don't want to live bound by fear.

I cast every anxious thought onto You right now. Take the burdens I cannot carry. Replace my restlessness with Your peace. Calm my heart, steady my breathing, and renew my mind.
When my mind feels loud, and my spirit feels weak, quiet me with Your love.

Remind me that I am not powerless Your Spirit within me is stronger than my fears. Help me to rest in the truth that You are working all things for my good. Holy Spirit, fill every anxious place with Your perfect love. Drive out fear, doubt, and panic with Your power. Let Your Word anchor me when emotions try to pull me under. Teach me to find stillness in Your presence, even when life feels uncertain.

I declare today that anxiety will not rule me, Your peace will. I choose to walk in faith, not fear. Thank You, Lord, that You care for me, that You hear me, and that You will never let me go. In Jesus' name, Amen.

Prayer for Healing a Broken Heart

"He heals the brokenhearted and binds up their wounds." Psalm 147:3

Lord,

My heart feels shattered into pieces. Betrayal, loss, disappointment, it all hurts so deeply. Father, You see every tear I cry in silence.

Please, heal my broken heart. Bind up the wounds no one else can see. Fill the empty spaces with Your love. Remind me that I am not abandoned, even when I feel alone.

When memories return and pain resurfaces, hold me close, Lord. Remind me that healing is a process, not a moment. Replace the ache of what I've lost with the peace of knowing You are still writing my story. Father, restore my joy where sorrow has taken root.

Teach me to find beauty again, in laughter, in stillness, and in hope. Let Your presence be the balm that soothes what others cannot touch. Show me that brokenness is not the end, but the place where Your grace begins to rebuild.

Father, help me to forgive the one who hurt me. Take away the bitterness trying to grow inside me. Give me courage to open my heart again, not in fear, but in trust of Your goodness.

Thank You that You are close to the brokenhearted. I may be broken today, but I will not stay broken. Your love is mending me piece by piece. In Jesus' name, Amen.

Prayer for Loneliness

"God sets the lonely in families." – Psalm 68:6

Father in heaven,
The nights feel so long when I am alone. The silence in my home can feel deafening. Lord, I long for companionship, for someone to talk to, to laugh with, to share life with.
Remind me that I am never truly alone. You are with me. Even in my solitude, You sit beside me. Fill my heart with Your presence until it overflows. When the emptiness feels heavy and tears come without reason, wrap me in Your peace. Let Your love be the warmth that fills every quiet corner. Whisper to my soul that I am seen, known, and deeply loved by You.

Father, help me to see this season not as punishment but as preparation. Teach me to find beauty in stillness, to hear Your voice in the quiet, and to discover who I am in You. Let this time draw me closer to Your heart and strengthen my faith.

Send the right people into my life, true friends, encouragers, and community. Remove the ache of isolation and replace it with comfort. Surround me with relationships that reflect Your love and kindness.

Lord, let me use this season of loneliness to grow closer to You. Teach me to lean into Your love until my heart is full. Thank You for being my constant companion, my healer, and my truest friend.
In Jesus' name, Amen.

Prayer for Overcoming Fear

"For God has not given us a spirit of fear, but of power and of love and of a sound mind." – 2 Timothy 1:7

Abba Father,
Fear has tried to grip me, fear of failure, fear of rejection, fear of the unknown. But Lord, You did not give me this spirit of fear. You gave me power, love, and a sound mind.
I reject fear in Jesus' name. I will not be paralyzed by what-ifs. I choose to trust that You are with me and that nothing takes You by surprise.

When fear whispers that I am not enough, remind me that You are my strength. Let Your perfect love drives out every trace of fear. Fill me with boldness to walk into the places You have called me, even when I cannot see what lies ahead. Father, speak peace to the storms that rise within me. Remind me that You are greater than the battles I face.

When anxiety tries to steal my breath, let Your Spirit breathe calm and confidence into my soul. Give me the courage to step forward, even trembling. Let faith rise louder than fear. Remind me that I am safe in Your hands.

Thank You, Lord, for freedom from fear. I walk boldly in Your strength. I rest in Your promises and find confidence in Your presence. In Jesus' name, Amen.

Prayer for Self-Control

"Like a city whose walls are broken through is a person who lacks self-control." – Proverbs 25:28

Creator,

I admit I struggle with self-control, over my words, my habits, and my desires. Sometimes I give in too easily and regret it later. Father, I do not want to be ruled by impulses but led by Your Spirit.

Strengthen me, Lord. Teach me to pause before I act, to think before I speak, and to resist temptation when it comes. Let Your Spirit rise up in me, giving me discipline, patience, and focus.

Father, fill me with a hunger for righteousness that outweighs the pull of temporary desires. Give me the strength to turn away from what harms me and the wisdom to pursue what honors You. Help me to master my habits instead of being mastered by them.

Rebuild the walls of my life where they have been broken down. Restore my integrity, renew my mind, and remind me that true freedom comes from surrender to You.

I thank You for giving me the fruit of self-control through Your Spirit. I claim it today. I choose to walk in obedience, discipline, and grace. In Jesus' name, Amen.

Prayer for Peace of Mind

"You will keep in perfect peace those whose minds are steadfast, because they trust in You." – Isaiah 26:3

Father God,

My thoughts run wild with worry, replaying every mistake, every fear, every uncertainty. Lord, I long for peace of mind.

Settle my spirit. Quiet the noise inside my head. Teach me to fix my thoughts on You, not on my problems. Replace my racing thoughts with steady trust.

When anxiety rises like a storm, speak peace over my heart. Remind me that Your voice is stronger than my fears. Help me to breathe deeply in Your presence and release the weight I was never meant to carry. Let Your Spirit be the calm that settles every restless thought.

Father, fill me with the assurance that I am never alone. Even in the stillness of night when my mind refuses to rest, be my comfort and my anchor. Surround me with Your presence until fear fades and faith remains.

Let Your perfect peace guard my heart and mind. Remind me that You are in control, even when everything feels uncertain. I choose to trust You with my mind and my future.

Thank You, Lord, that peace is mine because You promised it. I receive it now. May Your peace flow through me like a gentle river that never runs dry. In Jesus' name, Amen.

Prayer for Forgiveness Toward Self & Others

Forgive us our debts, as we also have forgiven our debtors." (Matthew 6:12)

Father in heaven,

I've been holding onto unforgiveness toward others, as well as toward myself. The pain, the regret, the anger they weigh me down and steal my peace. Father, I choose today to forgive. Not because they deserve it, but because I need freedom. Heal the bitterness in my heart and replace it with Your love. Teach me to see others through Your eyes, with compassion and grace.

And Lord, help me forgive myself. Remind me that Your mercy is new every morning and that Your grace covers all my failures. I don't have to live in guilt when You've already forgiven me. Help me walk in the freedom and peace that come from Your forgiveness.

I declare I am free from unforgiveness. My heart is light, my spirit restored, and my mind renewed. Thank You, Father, for the power of forgiveness and for loving me even when I fall short. In Jesus' name, Amen.

Prayer for Joy to Return

"Weeping may endure for a night, but joy comes in the morning."
Psalm 30:5

Father God,

My joy has felt stolen. Life's struggles have dimmed my laughter and silenced my song. But Lord, I believe Your promise joy will come again.
Restore joy to my heart. Let me smile without forcing it, laugh without faking it, and rejoice without hesitation. Replace heaviness with lightness, sorrow with gladness.

Lord, help me to see the blessings I've overlooked. Teach me to celebrate small victories, to notice daily mercies, and to live with gratitude.

Father, I declare that my joy is returning. The night is ending, and morning is breaking with new hope. Thank You for joy unspeakable, full of glory. In Jesus' name, Amen.

PART SEVEN

FAITH & SPIRITUAL GROWTH

Prayer for Restoration of Faith

"Now faith is the substance of things hoped for, the evidence of things not seen." – Hebrews 11:1

Lord,
I confess my faith has grown weak. I have prayed and waited, but sometimes it feels like You are silent. Doubt has crept in, and hope feels distant. Father, restore my faith.

Remind me that faith is not about what I see but about trusting who You are. Strengthen me when I feel weary and help me believe even when the evidence seems against me. When fear whispers that nothing will change, let Your Word speak louder. Remind me of the times You have come through before. Let memories of Your faithfulness become fuel for my faith today. Teach me to hold on to Your promises even when my heart feels heavy.

Father, renew the joy of my salvation and awaken my spirit again. Let Your presence reignite the fire within me. Turn my doubts into declarations of trust and my weakness into worship. Show me that You are working behind the scenes even when I cannot see it.
Lord, bring back the fire I once had, the passion to pray, to worship, to trust without hesitation. Remove the heaviness of unbelief and replace it with the light of faith.

I declare today that my faith is being restored, not by my own strength but by Your Spirit working in me. Thank You, Father, for never letting me go. Amen.

Prayer for Strength to Pray Again

"Pray without ceasing." – 1 Thessalonians 5:17

Father God,

There are days I do not even have the words to pray. My heart is heavy, my spirit tired. But Lord, I want to talk to You again. I want my prayer life restored.

Help me push past discouragement. Remind me that prayer does not have to be perfect, it just has to be real. Lord, let my first words be honest cries from my heart.

When my faith feels small, remind me that even a whisper reaches Your throne. Teach me that You treasure sincerity more than eloquence. Let me feel Your nearness when I sit in silence, knowing that You understand every unspoken word.

Breathe fresh life into my prayer time. Give me discipline when I want to quit and joy when I come into Your presence. Teach me to pray not just for blessings, but to know You more deeply.

Father, lift the weight of guilt that has silenced my voice. Replace it with grace and confidence to approach You boldly. Restore my hunger to seek You, to pour out my heart, and to listen for Your gentle voice again.

Thank You, Father, for always listening, even when my prayers have been whispers. Thank You for never turning away. Draw me close again and fill me with the strength to pray. In Jesus' name, Amen.

Prayer for Guidance in Confusion

"Trust in the Lord with all your heart, and lean not on your own understanding; in all your ways acknowledge Him, and He will direct your paths." – Proverbs 3:5–6

Lord,

Right now, I feel confused. There are so many choices, and I don't know which way to go. I don't want to lean on my own understanding; I need Your wisdom.

Father, speak clearly to me. Open the right doors and shut the wrong ones. Place peace in my heart when I'm walking in Your will, and unease when I'm straying from it.

Help me to trust You even when the path ahead looks uncertain. Remind me that You see the bigger picture and that Your ways are higher than mine.

Thank You, Lord, for being my guide, my compass, and my counselor. In Jesus' name, Amen.

Prayer for a Closer Walk with God

"Draw near to God, and He will draw near to you."
James 4:8

Father in Heaven,

I want to be closer to You. I don't want a shallow faith. long for a deeper relationship with You that shapes my thoughts, words, and actions. Lord, help me remove distractions that pull me away from You and quiet the noise that competes for my attention.

Teach me to seek You first in my mornings and rest in You at night. Give me a hunger for Your Word, a passion for prayer, and a joy for worship that fills my heart with peace. Help me to recognize Your voice and follow Your leading in every decision I make.

Lord, reveal Yourself to me in new and beautiful ways. Let me feel Your presence daily, not just on Sundays. Teach me to walk with You like a friend, sharing every part of my life the joys, the struggles, and the in-between moments.

When I wander, draw me back. When I grow weary, renew my strength. When I am unsure, remind me that You are near and that Your love never changes.

Thank You for always waiting for me to draw near. I'm coming back, Lord, ready to walk hand in hand with You.
 In Jesus' name, Amen.

Prayer for Hearing God's Voice

"My sheep listen to my voice; I know them, and they follow me." (John 10:27)

God in Heaven,
Sometimes I wonder if I'm hearing You or just my own thoughts. I long to know Your voice more clearly. Teach me to recognize when You are speaking.

Quiet the noise of fear, doubt, and distraction. Tune my spirit to hear Your whispers through Your Word, through prayer, and through Your Spirit.

Lord, confirm Your voice with peace that passes understanding. Help me not just to hear, but to obey quickly, without hesitation or fear. When I am uncertain, remind me that You are patient and kind, always guiding me with love. Let Your Word be the lamp that lights my path and Your Spirit the gentle breeze that directs my steps.

Thank You that You are a speaking God. Let my ears be attentive, my heart open, and my spirit ready to follow wherever You lead. In Jesus' name, Amen.

Prayer for Returning to Church

"For where two or three are gathered in My name, there am I among them." — Matthew 18:20

Our Father who art in Heaven,
I admit I've drifted from church. Hurt, busyness, and disappointment have kept me away. But Lord, I know I need the fellowship of believers. Heal my wounds from past church experiences. Remove bitterness and give me courage to try again. Lead me to a church family where I can worship freely, grow spiritually, and serve faithfully.

Lord, remind me that the church is not perfect, but it is Your design. Help me be part of the solution, not the problem. Restore in me the joy of gathering with others in Your name.

Renew my desire to be planted in Your house, where roots of faith can grow deep and strong. Let Your Spirit draw me back into community, where love, accountability, and encouragement abound.

Thank You, Father, for welcoming me back into Your house and into the warmth of Your people. Strengthen my heart to remain faithful and connected. In Jesus' name, Amen.

Prayer for Spiritual Hunger

"Blessed are those who hunger and thirst for righteousness, for they shall be filled." Matthew 5:6

Creator God,
I don't want to be lukewarm in my faith. Stir up a hunger in me for more of You. Let me thirst for Your Word, crave Your presence, and long for righteousness.

Father, break every distraction that dulls my appetite for You. Take away complacency and replace it with passion. Let my soul be unsatisfied until it is filled with You.

Lord, fill me with fresh fire. Let my hunger for You grow stronger each day. Teach me to delight in Your truth and to find my deepest joy in Your nearness. Remind me that nothing in this world can satisfy like You can.

Renew my heart, Lord. Let every moment draw me closer to You. Thank You for promising to satisfy those who seek after You. In Jesus' name, Amen.

Prayer for Trusting God Again

"Blessed is the one who trusts in the Lord, whose confidence is in Him."
Jeremiah 17:7

Father in Heaven,
I've been disappointed before, and it's made it hard to trust again. Sometimes I wonder why things didn't work out, and my heart hesitates to believe.

But Lord, I don't want to live in doubt. Teach me to trust You fully, even when I don't understand. Remind me of the times You've been faithful before.

Heal my heart from disappointment and strengthen my confidence in You. Help me believe that You are good, even when life feels hard.
When fear tries to whisper that things will never change, remind me that You are still in control. When worry clouds my thoughts, fill me with Your peace that surpasses all understanding.

Let my trust in You grow stronger each day. Teach me to rest in Your timing, knowing that every promise You make is sure and every plan You have is good.

Father, I choose to place my trust in You again today. Hold my heart steady in faith and help me walk with quiet confidence in Your love, In Jesus' name, Amen.

Prayer for Overcoming Doubt

"Immediately the father of the child cried out and said, 'I believe; help my unbelief!" Mark 9:24

Our Father in heaven,
I believe in You, but sometimes doubt creeps in. I question if You hear me, if You care, if You will answer. Father, help my unbelief.
Strengthen my faith where it is weak. Remind me that doubt does not disqualify me but is an opportunity for me to lean on You more.

Father, I bring my doubts into the light. Meet me in my questions and replace them with confidence in Your Word.
Teach me to rest in Your promises even when I cannot see the outcome.
Let my heart be still in the knowledge that You are faithful and good.
When I cannot trace Your hand, help me trust Your heart.

Thank You for being patient with me, even when I struggle to believe.
Thank You for never turning away from me but drawing me closer with love that never fails.
In Jesus' name, Amen.

Prayer for Lasting Hope

"But those who hope in the Lord will renew their strength; they will soar on wings like eagles." (Isaiah 40:31)

Father God,

Sometimes hope feels like it slips through my fingers. Life's challenges weigh heavily, and I feel weary. But Lord, You are the God of hope. Renew my strength today. Lift me on eagle's wings above discouragement. Let me see my situation through Your eyes. Remind me that hope in You is never wasted.

When my heart feels heavy, breathe new life into my spirit. Help me to remember that Your promises never fail, even when I cannot see the way forward. Teach me to rest in Your timing and trust that You are working all things for my good.

Lord, anchor my hope not in people, money, or circumstances, but in You alone. Fill me with joy and peace as I trust in You.

I declare that my hope is alive, strong, and lasting because it is rooted in You.

Thank You, Lord, for being my constant light when all else fades. In Jesus' name, Amen.

PART EIGHT

CHURCH & COMMUNITY

Prayer for Pastors and Leaders

"Remember your leaders, those who spoke to you the word of God. Consider the outcome of their way of life and imitate their faith." Hebrews 13:7

Lord Jesus,

I lift my pastor and leaders before You. Father, they carry so many burdens that I cannot see. They preach, they guide, they pray, yet sometimes they are weary and in need of strength themselves.

Cover them with Your protection. Guard their families, their health, and their minds. Give them wisdom to lead with love, courage to stand in truth, and humility to serve faithfully.

Lord, when they feel unappreciated, remind them that their labor is not in vain. Surround them with support, encouragement, and Godly friendships. Let no weapon formed against them prosper.

Father, bless my pastor and leaders abundantly. Refresh them with Your Spirit so they can continue to pour out to others. Renew their vision and fill their hearts with joy in serving You. Remind them daily that they are chosen and deeply loved.

May their words be filled with grace and power, their hearts anchored in peace, and their lives be a living testimony of Your faithfulness. Strengthen their hands for the work ahead and let their ministries bear lasting fruit for Your glory. In Jesus' name, Amen.

Prayer for Unity in the Church

"Make every effort to keep the unity of the Spirit through the bond of peace." Ephesians 4:3

Lord,

I bring my church family before You. Too often, we allow differences and disagreements to divide us. Father, I ask for unity.

Heal wounds caused by gossip, pride, and misunderstandings. Remind us that we are one body with many parts, and each part is valuable in Your eyes. Teach us to honor and listen to one another with humility and grace.

Let love be our foundation and peace be our bond. Help us focus on what unites us in Christ Jesus rather than what separates us. May we learn to celebrate diversity within our fellowship as a reflection of Your creative design.

Father, may our church be a living example of unity in a divided world. Let our worship be filled with harmony and our service overflow with compassion. Bind us together with cords that cannot be broken. Strengthen our hearts to seek reconciliation quickly and to forgive freely, just as You have forgiven us. In Jesus' name, Amen.

Prayer Against Division and Gossip

"Without wood a fire goes out; without a gossip a quarrel dies down." – Proverbs 26:20

Father in Heaven,

Division and gossip have caused harm in the church. Lord, I confess my own part in conversations I should not have entertained. Please forgive me.

Protect our church from the spirit of division. Silence every gossiping tongue. Let truth, grace, and love guard our words.

Teach me to speak life, not rumors, encouragement, not criticism. Help me to be a peacemaker, not a divider. Fill my heart with humility and compassion so that I may build others up instead of tearing them down. Lord, cleanse Your house. Let our church be marked by love, not slander. Unite us by Your Spirit and remind us that we are one body under Christ. May our fellowship reflect Your heart of peace and forgiveness. In Jesus' name, Amen.

Prayer for Church Growth

"And the Lord added to their number daily those who were being saved." (Acts 2:47)

Father God,
I pray for my church to grow, not just in numbers, but in spirit, love, and discipleship. Lord, draw the lost to our doors and open their hearts to receive Your truth. Use us to reach our community with the Gospel and let Your presence fill every gathering.

Give us creativity in outreach, boldness in evangelism, and compassion in service. Let our love for one another be the testimony that draws people to You. May every ministry flourish, every member be strengthened, and every visitor encounter Your grace and peace.

Father, remove every hindrance to growth, fear, complacency, pride, or division. Unite us in purpose and ignite a passion for revival within our hearts. Let the fire of Your Spirit fall upon us so that souls are saved, families are restored, and lives are transformed by Your power.
Thank You, Lord, for building Your church. We trust that the gates of hell will not prevail against it. May we be faithful stewards of the harvest You send. In Jesus' name, Amen.

Prayer for Revival

"Will You not revive us again, that Your people may rejoice in You?" – Psalm 85:6

Dear Heavenly Father,
My heart longs for revival in my church, in my community, in my city.
Father, let Your Spirit fall fresh on us. Awaken our hearts to love You more deeply.

Break complacency, ignite passion, and stir hunger for Your presence.
Let miracles, signs, and wonders follow as we return to You with surrendered hearts.

Breathe life into dry bones, Lord. Restore joy where there has been weariness, and faith where there has been doubt. Let forgiveness flow freely, and unity rise among Your people.

May Your Word burn within us again, leading us to holiness, compassion, and boldness.
Lord, begin revival in me. Set my heart on fire, so that I can be part of what You are doing in my church.

Let my life shine as a living testimony of Your power and love.
Thank You for hearing this cry. I believe revival is coming, not by might, nor by power, but by Your Spirit. In Jesus' name, Amen.

Prayer for Outreach & Missions

"Go therefore and make disciples of all nations." – Matthew 28:19

Father in Heaven,

You commanded us to go into all the world, but sometimes we are hesitant. Lord, give our church a heart for outreach and missions.

Open our eyes to the needs in our own neighborhood and across the world. Provide resources, courage, and creativity to spread the Gospel.

Send us where others won't go. Use our hands to serve, our mouths to speak, and our hearts to love.

Let compassion move us and let Your Spirit lead us. May we be bold in proclaiming Your truth, steadfast in prayer, and generous in love.

Father, bless every missionary and every outreach team, those near and far. Strengthen them when they grow weary, protect them from harm, and remind them that their labor in the Lord is not in vain.

Unite us as one body, working together to make Your name known among all peoples. Let us be faithful to the call to go and make disciples, until every nation hears the good news of Jesus Christ. In His mighty name we pray, Amen.

Prayer for Church Finances

"And my God will meet all your needs according to the riches of His glory in Christ Jesus." - Philippians 4:19

Lord Jesus,
You see the financial needs of our church: the bills, the outreach efforts, the ministries, and the missions. Father, provide abundantly for Your house.

Bless every giver with provision, and stir generosity in the hearts of Your people. Teach us to trust You with our tithes and offerings.
Lord, let there be no lack in Your house. Multiply every resource so that the ministry can flourish and the Gospel can spread. Let every seed sown bear fruit that lasts, touching lives and advancing Your Kingdom.

Grant wisdom to those who steward these finances. Help them to manage every resource with integrity, vision, and faith. May our church always be known for generosity, faithfulness, and compassion toward others.

Thank You for being the God who supplies all our needs, who opens doors no one can shut, and who blesses far beyond what we could ask or imagine. In Jesus' name, Amen.

Prayer for Youth in the Church

"Don't let anyone look down on you because you are young, but set an example for the believers." – 1 Timothy 4:12

Father God,

I lift up the young people in my church. Lord, they face temptations and pressures every day. Strengthen their faith and help them to stand firm in Your truth.

Let them be bold for You, unashamed of the Gospel. Surround them with mentors and leaders who will guide them in wisdom and love. Protect them from destructive influences and ignite a deep passion in their hearts to serve You wholeheartedly.

Father, let revival begin with the youth. Fill them with Your Spirit so that they may be lights in their schools, communities, and families. Use them as leaders, worshippers, and witnesses of Your grace. May their lives reflect Your goodness and draw others closer to You.

Thank You for raising up a generation on fire for You. Help them to walk in purity, purpose, and power. In Jesus' name, Amen.

Prayer for Healing Among Believers

"Bear one another's burdens, and so fulfill the law of Christ."
– Galatians 6:2

Lord Almighty,
I pray for healing in our church family. Some are wounded by loss, some by illness, and others by disappointment. Father, pour out Your comfort and healing upon each heart.

Teach us to bear one another's burdens, to pray faithfully for each other, and to walk together in love. Remove judgment and replace it with compassion. Where there is division, bring unity. Where there is weariness, bring renewal.

Let our church be a hospital for the hurting, a place where broken hearts are mended, faith is strengthened, and souls are restored. May Your Spirit move among us with power and tenderness, bringing peace, restoration, and hope.

Thank You, Lord, for healing among us and for the love that binds us together as one family in Christ. In Jesus' name, Amen.

Prayer for God's Presence in Worship

"God is spirit, and His worshipers must worship in the Spirit and in truth." — John 4:24

Father God,

I don't want worship to be routine or empty. Lord, let Your presence fill our services and our homes. Break through our singing with Your Spirit's power and move among us in ways only You can.

Let worship be more than songs; let it be surrender. Touch every heart, heal every soul, and restore every spirit as we lift Your name high. May Your glory fall in this place and remind us that You alone are worthy.

Father, remove distractions and open our hearts to hear You clearly. Remind us why we worship, to glorify You and draw closer to Your heart. Thank You that when we draw near in worship, You draw near to us.

Fill our gatherings with awe, unity, and love. Let our worship please You and transform us to reflect Your goodness in all we do. In Jesus' name, Amen.

PART NINE

HEALING & DELIVERANCE

Prayer for Healing from Illness

"But He was wounded for our transgressions, He was bruised for our iniquities… and by His stripes we are healed." – Isaiah 53:5

Father God,
You see the sickness in my body, the weakness that drains me. Some days I feel so tired, I wonder if I will ever be whole again. But Lord, I believe You are the Great Physician.

Touch me with Your healing hand. Restore every cell, every organ, every system in my body. Remove pain, disease, and infirmity. Let Your healing flow through me from the top of my head to the soles of my feet. Father, when fear rises in me, remind me that by Jesus' stripes I am healed. Strengthen my faith to hold onto Your promise, even when symptoms remain. Fill my heart with peace instead of worry, and hope instead of despair. Help me to rest in Your love and trust that You are working, even in the waiting.

Surround me with Your presence, Lord. Let Your Spirit breathe life and renewal into every part of me, body, mind, and soul. May my healing be a testimony of Your goodness and mercy, bringing glory to Your name. Thank You for being my healer. I declare healing, restoration, and strength over my life, in Jesus' mighty name, Amen.

Prayer for Mental Health Healing

"For God has not given us a spirit of fear, but of power and of love and of a sound mind." – 2 Timothy 1:7

Lord God Almighty,
My mind feels like a battlefield. Anxiety, depression, and racing thoughts wear me down. Father, I need Your healing in my mind.

Silence the lies of the enemy. Replace fear with peace, confusion with clarity, and despair with hope. Restore balance, joy, and calmness.
Lord, renew my mind with Your Word. Teach me to dwell on what is true, noble, and praiseworthy. Help me to recognize when my thoughts drift toward darkness and gently guide me back to Your light. Surround me with Your presence when I feel alone and remind me that You are my refuge and strength, an ever-present help in times of trouble.

Send people into my life who will encourage and support me in this journey. Grant me the courage to seek help when I need it, and the grace to rest when my soul feels weary. Let Your Holy Spirit be the calm in my storm and the voice that whispers peace into my heart.

Father, I receive Your promise of a sound mind. I choose to trust You even when I don't understand. Thank You for healing and restoring me mentally, emotionally, and spiritually. In Jesus' name, Amen.

Prayer for Deliverance from Addictions

"So if the Son sets you free, you will be free indeed."
– John 8:36

Father God,

I'm tired of being bound by this addiction. It feels stronger than me, and I've failed so many times trying to break free. But Lord, I believe nothing is stronger than You.

Break these chains that have held me captive. Destroy the cravings, the triggers, the habits that keep me stuck. Replace my desire for this addiction with a hunger for You.

Father, when temptation comes, give me strength to resist. Surround me with people who will hold me accountable and speak life into me. Remind me daily that my identity is not in my past or my struggles, but in who I am in Christ, redeemed, forgiven, and loved beyond measure. Heal the wounds in my heart that led me here, Lord. Fill every empty place with Your peace, Your presence, and Your purpose. Teach me to depend on Your Spirit and to find joy in Your Word.

I declare today that I am free, not because of my willpower, but because the Son has set me free. And whom the Son sets free is free indeed. Thank You for Your mercy, Your patience, and Your deliverance.
In Jesus' mighty name, Amen.

Prayer for Breaking Generational Curses

"Christ redeemed us from the curse of the law by becoming a curse for us." – Galatians 3:13

Lord Jesus,
I see patterns in my family: anger, addiction, divorce, and poverty, and I don't want them passed down to my children. Father, I ask You to break every generational curse over my bloodline.

Through the blood of Jesus, I declare freedom. Every curse is broken, every chain destroyed. What plagued past generations will not continue in mine. The power of the cross stands between my family and every dark pattern.

Father, replace curses with blessings. Let love, faith, peace, and prosperity flow through my family tree. Where there was strife, bring unity. Where there was lack, bring abundance. Where there was pain, bring healing and joy.

May my children and their children walk in freedom and not bondage. Let the story of my family line be rewritten by Your grace and mercy. Thank You, Lord, for redeeming my family through Christ. Thank You for turning every curse into a testimony of Your power and goodness. In Jesus' mighty name, Amen.

Prayer for Healing in Grief and Loss

"Blessed are those who mourn, for they shall be comforted." – Matthew 5:4

My Father in Heaven

My heart aches with grief. The loss feels unbearable, and sometimes I don't know how to go on. Lord, comfort me as only You can.

Wipe away my tears. Hold me in my pain. Remind me that even in sorrow, You are near. Teach me that grieving doesn't mean I lack faith, but that I loved deeply.

Father, help me honor the memory of the one I've lost while still choosing to live fully. Let Your presence be my comfort through the long nights and empty days. When the ache returns, whisper peace to my soul. Help me find moments of gratitude even in the shadow of loss.

Renew my strength each morning, Lord, and guide me to hope again. Teach me to trust that You are healing my heart, little by little, even when I cannot see it. Let Your love be the light that carries me forward until joy returns in its quiet, gentle way. Thank You for being close to the brokenhearted. In Jesus' name, Amen.

Prayer for Healing in Grief and Loss

"Blessed are those who mourn, for they shall be comforted." Matthew 5:4

Heavenly Father,

My heart aches with grief. The loss feels unbearable, and sometimes I don't know how to go on. Lord, comfort me as only You can.

Wipe away my tears. Hold me in my pain. Remind me that even in sorrow, You are near. Teach me that grieving doesn't mean I lack faith, but that I loved deeply.

Father, help me honor the memory of the one I've lost while still choosing to live fully. Let Your presence be my comfort through the long nights and empty days.

Give me strength to take one step at a time, and the courage to face each new day with grace. When memories flood my heart, let them bring peace instead of pain.

Help me trust that You are working even in this loss, turning ashes into beauty in ways I cannot yet see.

Thank You for being close to the brokenhearted, and for promising eternal life where all tears will be wiped away. In Jesus' name, Amen.

Prayer for Restoration After Divorce

"The Lord is near to the brokenhearted and saves the crushed in spirit."
– Psalm 34:18

Dear God,

Divorce has left me broken, rejected, and weary. The dreams I had for marriage feel shattered. But Father, I believe You can restore me.

Heal my heart from bitterness and regret. Teach me to forgive myself and my former spouse. Remove the shame and replace it with hope.

Father, restore my confidence, my joy, and my trust in You. Remind me that my identity is not defined by divorce but by being Your beloved child.

Help me to see that even in loss, You are writing a new story for my life. Give me strength to walk forward, trusting that Your plans for me are still good.

When loneliness tries to overtake me, remind me of Your constant presence. When fear whispers that I will never love or be whole again, speak Your truth over me, that I am seen, chosen, and deeply loved.

Lord, rebuild my life. What feels like the end is not the end with You. Bring beauty from these ashes and peace to my soul. In Jesus' name, Amen.

Prayer for Physical Strength & Energy

"But those who hope in the Lord will renew their strength. They will soar on wings like eagles." Isaiah 40:31

Father God,

My body feels tired, weak, and worn out. Sometimes even the simplest tasks drain me. Lord, renew my strength.

Fill me with energy, vitality, and health. Help me care for my body as Your temple. Strengthen me so I can fulfill the assignments You've given me.

When I feel weary, help me remember that You are my source of life and power. Let Your Spirit breathe new life into me, reviving every weary muscle, calming every anxious thought, and renewing my mind with peace.

Lord, when fatigue overwhelms me, remind me that Your strength is made perfect in weakness. Teach me to rest in You, trusting that Your grace is enough for every moment.

I choose to hope in You today. May Your joy become my strength, and may my heart overflow with gratitude even in moments of exhaustion. Thank You, Father, for renewing my strength like the eagle's and lifting me to soar above weariness. In Jesus' name, Amen.

Prayer for Peace After Trauma

"You will keep him in perfect peace, whose mind is stayed on You, because he trusts in You." Isaiah 26:3

Lord,

The trauma I went through still lingers in my mind. Flashbacks, fear, and pain try to hold me captive. But Father, I believe You can give me peace.

Heal the memories that torment me. Calm my mind when fear rises. Replace nightmares with restful sleep. Guard my thoughts with Your perfect peace.

When I feel broken, remind me that You are near to the brokenhearted. When I feel weak, remind me that Your strength is made perfect in my weakness. Let Your love fill every place where fear once lived.

Father, let me not live as a victim but as a victor in Christ. Use my story not for shame, but as a testimony of Your healing power. May my pain become purpose, my sorrow become song, and my scars become signs of Your faithfulness.

Thank You, Lord, for peace that surpasses understanding, for holding me when I can't hold myself, and for turning ashes into beauty. In Jesus' name, Amen.

Prayer for Deliverance from Spiritual Attacks

"No weapon formed against you shall prosper." Isaiah 54:17

Father God,

I come before You in humility and trust. I feel under spiritual attack. The enemy whispers lies, stirs confusion, and tries to steal my peace. But Lord, I know that no weapon formed against me shall prosper, for You are my refuge and my shield.

Cover me with the blood of Jesus and place Your hedge of protection around me. Surround me with Your mighty angels, encamping about me and my household. Break every curse, rebuke every demonic assignment, and silence every voice of the enemy that speaks against Your truth.

Fill me with courage, boldness, and discernment. Strengthen my spirit to resist temptation and stand firm in Your Word. Let my prayers become weapons of warfare that push back darkness, releasing Your light, peace, and power into every area of my life.

Father, I lift up my heart in worship, knowing You are greater than every battle I face. I declare victory in Jesus' name, over my mind, my family, my health, and my destiny. The enemy is defeated, and I am free to walk in Your promises.

Thank You, Lord, for Your unfailing love and protection. I stand in faith, clothed in the armor of God, and I will not be shaken. In Jesus' mighty name, Amen.

PART TEN

RESTORATION & BREAKTHROUGH

Prayer for Financial Restoration

Heavenly Father,

I come before You today with an open heart and trembling hands. Lord, You know the weight I've been carrying, the bills, the debts, the uncertainty about tomorrow. Sometimes the pressure feels overwhelming, and I confess that fear has tried to take root. But today, I lay it all down at Your feet, because You are my Provider, my Sustainer, and my Restorer.

Father, I remember Your Word in Philippians 4:19: "And my God shall supply all your needs according to His riches in glory by Christ Jesus." I declare this over my life right now. Not according to my job, not according to the economy, not according to my own strength, but according to Your riches in glory. And Lord, Your supply never runs dry.

Lord, I ask for forgiveness where I have mismanaged resources or allowed worry to consume me. Wash me clean and teach me to be a wise steward over all that You entrust to me. Father, I believe that You are opening doors of opportunity, doors no man can shut. I believe You are sending divine connections, unexpected blessings, and supernatural provision into my life.

Even in the waiting, I choose to trust You. Even when I don't see the numbers adding up, I will lift my eyes to the hills, knowing my help comes from You.

God, breathe fresh hope into my spirit. Restore what was lost, multiply what remains, and release me into overflow so that I may not only meet my needs but also bless others as a testimony of Your goodness.

Lord, I don't just ask for finances I ask for peace of mind, strength of heart, and faith that will not waver. Let this season of lack become a story of restoration, a testimony that will glorify Your name.

Thank You, Father, for hearing me, for loving me, and for being faithful. I receive by faith the financial restoration You have promised. And I stand on Your Word, declaring that lack has no place in my life because You are Jehovah Jireh, my provider. In Jesus' mighty name, Amen.

Prayer for Marriage Restoration

Heavenly Father,

I come before You today with a heart that is both heavy and hopeful. Lord, You know the struggles within my marriage, the distance, the wounds, the words that have cut deep. You see the silent tears and the unspoken pain. Yet, Father, I believe that what You have joined together, no one and nothing can tear apart (Mark 10:9)

Lord, I lift my marriage into Your hands. I ask for Your healing to flow into every broken place. Where there has been a misunderstanding, bring clarity. Where there has been anger, pour out patience. Where there has been hurt, let forgiveness rise like a river. Father, soften our hearts toward one another and remind us of the love that first brought us together.

Your Word declares in Joel 2:25: "I will restore to you the years that the locust has eaten." Lord, I claim this promise over my marriage. Restore the joy we once shared, the laughter, the intimacy, and the unity that felt unshakable. Replace bitterness with compassion, silence with communication, and fear with faith.

Father, I rebuke every scheme of the enemy that seeks to divide and destroy. I declare that my marriage is covered by the power of Jesus. Let our home be filled once more with peace, respect, and unconditional love. Teach us to pray together, to dream together, and to walk hand in hand again, not in our own strength, but in Yours.

Lord, heal us from the inside out. Make our marriage a testimony that with You, nothing is beyond repair. Let others see Your glory through our story of redemption.

I thank You in advance, Father, because I believe restoration is already in motion. I choose to stand on Your promises, trusting that You are doing a new thing. May this marriage be stronger than before, rooted deeply in You. In the mighty name of Jesus, Amen.

Prayer for Wayward Children's Return

Heavenly Father,

I lift up my child before You today with a heart that aches but refuses to give up hope. Lord, You see where they are, You know the path they've chosen, and You know the struggles that weigh them down. Even when they seem far from me, and even farther from You, I hold onto Your promise that You will never leave nor forsake them.

Lord, I cling to Your Word in Proverbs 22:6: "Train up a child in the way he should go, and when he is old he will not depart from it." I planted seeds of faith, and I believe those seeds are still alive, waiting for Your breath of life to make them grow again.

Father, call them back with Your love that never fails. Break through the noise of the world and whisper to their heart. Remove every distraction, every false friend, every chain that pulls them away from Your presence. Lord, just as the prodigal son came to his senses and returned home, I pray my child will rise up and say, "I will return to my Father" (Luke 15:17-18).

I ask You to protect them in their wandering. Place angels around them to guard their steps until they return. Give me patience in the waiting, compassion in the hurting, and faith that will not waver. Lord, heal the brokenness, restore the relationship, and let forgiveness flow freely when they come home.

Father, I declare that no matter how far they run, they cannot outrun Your grace. Your love is stronger than rebellion, Your mercy deeper than mistakes, and Your calling louder than the world's voice. I trust You to finish the good work You started in their life.

Thank You, Lord, for hearing this prayer. I wait with open arms, just as You do, believing that my wayward child will return, restored, renewed, and rooted in You. In Jesus' mighty name, Amen.

Prayer for Faith After Failure

Heavenly Father,

I come before You today feeling the weight of failure heavy on my shoulders. Lord, You know the mistakes I've made, the opportunities I've missed, and the ways I've fallen short. At times, shame whispers that I am unworthy, and fear tells me that I'll never rise again. But today, Father, I choose to silence those voices and listen to Yours, the voice that calls me beloved, redeemed, and forgiven.

Your Word in Micah 7:8 declares: "Do not rejoice over me, my enemy; when I fall, I will arise; when I sit in darkness, the Lord will be a light to me." Lord, I hold onto this promise. I may have fallen, but by Your grace, I will rise again. Where I see failure, You see a setup for a comeback. Where I see brokenness, You see a vessel You can use for Your glory.

Father, rebuild my faith where doubt has crept in. Remind me that my identity is not defined by my failures, but by Your love and the finished work of Christ on the cross. Teach me to see failure not as the end, but as a stepping stone toward growth, humility, and deeper trust in You.

Lord, help me to forgive myself, just as You have forgiven me. Heal the wounds in my heart that keep me bound to regret.

Open my eyes to the lessons in this season and give me the courage to move forward with renewed strength.

I declare that what the enemy meant for evil, You will turn for good. I will not stay down in despair, because Your Word says that the righteous may fall seven times but rise again (Proverbs 24:16). I rise today not in my own strength, but in Yours.

Thank You, Father, that failure does not have the final word; Jesus does. I step forward in faith, believing that my story is still being written and that Your plans for me are good. In Jesus' name, Amen.

Restoration After Betrayal

"The Lord is close to the brokenhearted and saves those who are crushed in spirit." Psalm 34:18

Lord,

Being betrayed by someone I trusted has left me shattered. Father, it hurts so deeply. I feel the weight of disappointment, confusion, and loss pressing on my heart. Yet even here, in this valley of pain, I know You are near. You see every tear that falls, and You understand the ache no one else can.

Heal the broken places within me, Lord. Where trust has been crushed, breathe new life. Where bitterness has begun to take root, plant seeds of grace instead. Take away the sting of betrayal and replace it with Your peace that surpasses all understanding.

Teach me, Father, how to forgive, not because the wound was small, but because I refuse to let it poison my spirit. Help me release the grip of resentment and surrender my pain into Your capable hands. Remind me that vengeance belongs to You, not to me.

Restore my confidence in people, Lord. Help me to discern wisely without growing cold or guarded. Let my heart remain open to love, friendship, and fellowship again. Remind me that while people may fail, You are forever faithful. You will never betray, abandon, or deceive me.

Lift me out of this pit of sorrow. Let Your light penetrate every shadow of doubt and fear. Replace my grief with joy, my anger with compassion, and my despair with hope. Teach me to see even this heartbreak as an opportunity for deeper dependence on You.

Lord, rebuild me from within. Use this pain to refine my character, strengthen my faith, and draw me closer to Your heart. May I emerge from this season not bitter, but better, more gentle, more merciful, more like Christ.

Thank You, Lord, that nothing is wasted in Your hands. Thank You for being my refuge, my defender, and my restorer. I trust that You are working all things for my good, even the ones that broke me. I choose to believe that beauty will rise from these ashes.
In Jesus' name, Amen.

Prayer for Career Breakthrough

Heavenly Father,

I come before You with a heart that longs for direction and a breakthrough in my career. Lord, You see the doors that have closed, the disappointments I've faced, and the seasons of waiting that have tested my patience. At times I've wondered if I've been forgotten, but today I declare that You are a God who never forgets His children.

Your Word declares in Jeremiah 29:11: "For I know the plans I have for you," declares the Lord, "plans to prosper you and not to harm you, plans to give you a hope and a future." Father, I cling to this promise right now. I believe that even when I cannot see the full picture, You are orchestrating my steps toward the purpose You designed for me.

Lord, I surrender my career, my ambitions, and my timeline into Your hands. Where I've been striving in my own strength, teach me to lean fully on You. Open the right doors that no man can shut, and close every door that is not aligned with Your will. Father, send divine opportunities, kingdom connections, and favor that surrounds me like a shield.

When discouragement tries to take root, remind me that You are my source, not my employer, not the economy, not my resume You alone are my Provider.

Let my gifts and talents make room for me, just as Your Word promises in Proverbs 18:16. Elevate me in Your timing, Lord, and let my promotion bring glory to Your name, not just success to my life.

Father, prepare me for the breakthrough I'm praying for. Shape my character, strengthen my faith, and sharpen my skills so that when the door opens, I am ready to walk through it with excellence and humility. Let my career not only bless me but also bless others and advance Your kingdom.

I thank You in advance for the testimonies that will come from this season. I believe that the delay is not denial, and that the breakthrough is on its way. Lord, I stand in faith, knowing You are faithful to complete what You have begun in the mighty name of Jesus, Amen.

Prayer for Community Transformation

Heavenly Father,

I lift up my community before You today, the streets, the families, the leaders, the children, and every soul within it. Lord, You see the brokenness, the division, the struggles, and the needs. But You also see the potential, the gifts, and the destinies planted here. Father, I believe that through Your Spirit, true transformation can come not just for one home, but for every heart in this place.

Your Word declares in 2 Chronicles 7:14: "If my people, who are called by my name, will humble themselves and pray and seek my face and turn from their wicked ways, then I will hear from heaven, and I will forgive their sin and will heal their land." Lord, we humble ourselves today. Heal our land. Heal our neighborhoods. Heal our community with Your mercy and power.

Father, raise up peacemakers where there is conflict, hope-bringers where there is despair, and light-bearers where darkness has tried to reign. Let love replace hatred, unity replace division, and truth silence every lie. Send revival, Lord, not just within the walls of the church but in the streets, in the schools, in the homes, and in the marketplace. Lord, bless our leaders with wisdom and integrity. Strengthen families with love and faithfulness. Protect our children from harm and shape them into future leaders who will carry Your name with honor.

Let businesses thrive with righteousness, let opportunities rise for the unemployed, and let compassion flow for the brokenhearted.

Father, let my community be known not for its struggles but for its transformation a place where Your Spirit dwells, where miracles happen, and where lives are changed. Just as Jesus declared in Matthew 5:14, "You are the light of the world. A city set on a hill cannot be hidden." Lord, make our community that shining city, a beacon of hope and a testimony of Your glory.

I thank You in advance for the renewal You are bringing. I believe hearts will be softened, lives will be restored, and this community will rise as a living testimony of Your goodness.
In Jesus' mighty name, Amen.

Prayer for Breakthrough of Faith

Mark 11:22–24 (NIV)

"Have faith in God," Jesus answered. "Truly I tell you, if anyone says to this mountain, 'Go, throw yourself into the sea,' and does not doubt in their heart but believes that what they say will happen, it will be done for them. Therefore, I tell you, whatever you ask for in prayer, believe that you have received it, and it will be yours."

Heavenly Father, in the mighty name of Jesus Christ of Nazareth, I come boldly before Your throne of grace. I thank You for Your unfailing love, Your mercy, and Your power that never fails. Today, I declare a breakthrough of faith in my life. Every doubt, fear, unbelief, and limitation is broken by the power of the Holy Spirit. Your Ruah. I receive the faith that moves mountains, the faith that trusts You completely, and the faith that stands firm no matter what I see or feel.

Lord, ignite my spirit with fresh fire. Let my heart be fully persuaded by Your Word, for You are not a man that You should lie. I decree that my faith is alive, strong, and unwavering. I walk by faith and not by sight. Every promise You have spoken over my life shall come to pass. I align my mind, soul, and spirit with heaven's truth. Sometimes my faith feels weak. I doubt, I worry, and I fear. But Lord, I want to trust You fully.

Give me breakthrough faith, the kind that believes even when I can't see. The kind that speaks life into dead situations. The kind that trusts Your timing and Your goodness, even in the waiting.

Remind me, Lord, that You are working behind the scenes, even when I can't perceive it. Let my heart rest in Your promises, knowing that You are faithful to complete what You have begun. Teach me to fix my eyes not on what is seen, but on what is eternal. Father, strengthen my spirit. Let my faith move mountains and open doors. Let it silence fear and replace anxiety with peace. Help me to walk boldly in confidence, knowing You go before me.

Thank You that You are faithful, even when I struggle to believe. Thank You for loving me through my doubts and drawing me closer in every season. By the authority of Jesus Christ, I step into divine confidence, supernatural trust, and victorious faith. I believe, I receive, and I declare it done in the powerful name of Jesus Christ of Nazareth Amen.

Prayer for Open Doors in Life

Heavenly Father,

I come before You today with a heart full of longing and faith. Lord, You see the places in my life where I feel stuck, the doors that seem locked, and the opportunities that feel out of reach. At times, it feels like I am pressing against walls that will not move, but today, I declare that You are the God who opens doors that no one can shut.

Your Word in Revelation 3:8 says: "See, I have placed before you an open door that no one can shut." Father, I stand on this promise right now. I believe that You are making a way where there seems to be no way. Where man says "impossible," You say, "possible." Where the world says "closed," You declare "open."

Lord, I surrender my plans, my timing, and my expectations into Your hands. Open the doors that lead me into my divine purpose. Open doors of opportunity, of favor, of provision, and of breakthrough. And, Father, close every door that is not meant for me, every counterfeit, every distraction, every path that leads away from Your will.

I pray for courage to walk through the doors You open. Remove fear, doubt, and hesitation from my heart.

Give me the wisdom to recognize the doors You are placing before me and the strength to step boldly into new seasons. Lord, align my steps with Your Word, because I know that the steps of the righteous are ordered by You (Psalm 37:23). Father, I declare that stagnation has no hold on me. Delay has no authority over me. I will not stay bound in closed places when You are calling me into open spaces. Let my life become a testimony of Your power to open doors at the right time, in the right way, for the right reasons.

Thank You, Lord, for the doors that are opening even now, for answered prayers, divine connections, and fresh opportunities. I believe by faith that this is my season of open doors, and I will walk in them with gratitude and boldness. In Jesus' mighty name, Amen.

Prayer for Urgent Miracles

Heavenly Father,

I come before You today with desperation in my soul and faith in my heart. Lord, I need You now. Not tomorrow, not next week, but right now. You are the God of miracles, the One who parts seas, heals the sick, raises the dead, and calls things that are not as though they were. Father, I believe You can move in my situation today.

Your Word says in Jeremiah 32:27: "I am the Lord, the God of all mankind. Is anything too hard for me?" Lord, I know the answer, nothing is too hard for You! So I bring my impossible before You, trusting that You can turn it around in an instant.

Father, I ask for a miracle where there has been delay. I ask for breakthrough where there has been blockage. I ask for healing where there has been pain, provision where there has been lack, and restoration where there has been loss. Lord, let the supernatural collide with the natural right now in my life.

Just as the woman with the issue of blood pressed through the crowd to touch the hem of Jesus' garment and was made whole (Mark 5:34), I press in by faith today. I reach out and declare that one touch from You is enough to change everything. Lord, speak the word and let the miracle manifest.

I pray with boldness because Your Word tells me in Ephesians 3:20 that You are able to do exceedingly, abundantly, above all I can ask or imagine. Father, do what only You can do. Let testimonies spring forth from this very moment, testimonies that bring glory to Your name and remind the world that You are still a miracle-working God.

Lord, I won't wait until the miracle shows up to give You praise. I thank You now, I worship You now, I believe now. Because even in the waiting, I know You are moving. In Jesus' mighty name, Amen.

Bonus Prayers

Prayer for Freedom from Drug Addiction

Heavenly Father,

I come before You today, broken and weary, but still holding on to hope. Lord, You see the battles I face, the chains that try to keep me bound, and the cravings that whisper lies to my soul. But today, I declare that I am Yours, and I will not be defined by addiction. I will be defined by Your love, Your power, and Your freedom.

Your Word reminds me in 1 Corinthians 6:19-20: "Do you not know that your bodies are temples of the Holy Spirit, who is in you, whom you have received from God? You are not your own; you were bought at a price. Therefore honor God with your bodies." Lord, I declare that my body is not a place for destruction, but a dwelling place for Your Spirit. Help me to honor You by breaking free from this cycle of drugs and dependence.

Father, I ask for supernatural strength to resist temptation when it rises. Replace every craving with a hunger for Your presence. Replace the urge to escape with the peace that comes only from You. When my mind is clouded, renew it with Your truth. When my body aches, fill it with Your healing power. And when my heart feels empty, overflow it with Your love.

Lord, surround me with people who will lift me up, not pull me down. Bring mentors, friends, and leaders who will walk with me in this journey of freedom.

Remove toxic influences, break every generational curse, and destroy every stronghold that has tried to claim my life.

Father, I believe in Your promise in John 8:36: "So if the Son sets you free, you will be free indeed." I receive that freedom right now, not tomorrow, not someday, but today. I declare that drugs no longer control me. Addiction no longer defines me. Jesus Christ is my Deliverer, and through Him, I am free.

Thank You, Lord, for never giving up on me. Thank You for loving me even in my darkest moments. And thank You for the new life I am stepping into, one day at a time, one prayer at a time, one victory at a time.

In Jesus' mighty name, Amen.
"The LORD is near to all who call on him, to all who call on him in truth." Psalm 145:18

Hymn

What a Friend We Have in Jesus

All our sins and griefs to bear!

What a privilege to carry

Everything to God in prayer!

Oh, what peace we often forfeit,

Oh, what needless pain we bear,

All because we do not carry

Everything to God in prayer.

Prayer for a Grieving Child

Heavenly Father,

I come to You with a heart that feels broken and heavy. I miss my mom/dad so much, and sometimes the sadness feels too big for me to carry. I don't always understand why this had to happen, but I know that You see me, You hear me, and You are close to me when I cry.

Lord, I ask You to hold me when I feel alone. Wrap me in Your love the way my parent used to. Let me feel Your presence beside me when the nights are quiet and the tears come. Remind me that I am never truly by myself, because You promised to never leave me nor forsake me.

Your word says in Psalm 34:18, "The Lord is close to the brokenhearted and saves those who are crushed in spirit." Father, I ask You to stay close to my broken heart. Heal the hurt little by little, and help me remember the good times with a smile instead of just tears.

Please give me comfort when I see other kids with their parents and feel that deep ache inside. Help me know that You are still writing my story, and that I am loved, chosen, and cared for. Protect me, guide me, and remind me that my parents' love lives on in me, and that one day, because of Jesus, there will be no more tears and no more goodbyes.

Lord, carry me through the days when I feel weak. Give me hope when I feel lost. Teach me to lean on You for strength and let Your peace guard my heart. Thank You for being my heavenly Father who never lets me go. In Jesus' name, I pray, Amen.

Prayer for a Parent with Dementia

Heavenly Father,

I lift up my parent to You right now. It hurts to see the changes in their mind, the forgetting, the confusion, and the moments when they don't seem like themselves. Lord, sometimes it breaks my heart, and I feel so helpless, but I know that nothing is too hard for You.

You created my parent. You know every hair on their head and every thought before it's even spoken. Even when their memory fades, You remember them perfectly. When they feel lost, You know exactly where they are. When they struggle to find words, You understand the cries of their heart.

Your word says in Isaiah 46:4, "Even to your old age and gray hairs I am He, I am He who will sustain you. I have made you and I will carry you; I will sustain you and I will rescue you." Lord, I claim that promise over my parent. Carry them through this season. Sustain them when their strength fails. Rescue their mind with Your peace and their heart with Your love.

Father, when I grow weary or frustrated, remind me to see them through Your eyes, with compassion, patience, and grace. Let me be a reflection of Your love to them in every moment, whether they recognize me or not.

I ask You to fill their days with comfort. Replace fear with peace, agitation with calm, and confusion with moments of joy. Surround them with caregivers, doctors, and loved ones who will treat them with dignity and kindness.

Lord, help me trust that even in this valley, You are walking beside us. Remind me that their life is still precious, their soul is still Yours, and their spirit is still deeply loved. Thank You for the gift of their life, and for the truth that You never forget Your children.

In Jesus' name, I pray amen.

Prayer for a Child Experiencing Mental Distress

Heavenly Father,

I come before You with a heart that feels broken and heavy for my child. Lord, I don't always understand why this has happened, but I know You are the God who sees, the God who heals, and the God who restores. My child is Yours, and even when their mind is troubled, their soul is held in Your hands.

Father, when I see the confusion, the fear, or the pain in their eyes, I ask You to step in with Your peace. Where there is chaos in their thoughts, speak Your order. Where there is torment, bring Your calm. Where there is darkness, let the light of Christ shine.

Your word says in 2 Timothy 1:7, "For God has not given us the spirit of fear, but of power, and of love, and of a sound mind." Lord, I hold onto that promise for my child. I speak life over their mind. I ask You to restore what has been broken, renew what has been damaged, and revive what feels lost.

When I grow tired, remind me that Your strength is made perfect in weakness. Teach me to love my child the way You love them, without condition, without giving up, and with hope that never fades. Lord, let me be an instrument of Your grace, patient and gentle even in the hardest moments.

Cover my child with Your protection. Guard his/her mind, his/her heart, and his/her spirit. Remind him/her, even in confusion, that they are not abandoned, that they are still deeply loved, and that You are near. Let Your presence go where my words cannot, bringing comfort and healing that only You can give.

I thank You, Lord, that nothing is impossible for You. You are the God who can speak peace to the storm, and I believe You can speak peace to my child's mind. I trust You with their life, and I trust You with mine. In Jesus' name, I pray, Amen.

Prayer for Healing from Family Hurt

Heavenly Father,

I come before You with an honest heart. Lord, I am hurting because of the words and actions of my family member. The pain runs deep, and sometimes it feels heavier because it comes from someone so close to me. I don't always know how to handle the emotions, anger, sadness, disappointment, but I know I can bring them to You.

Lord, You see the tears I have cried in secret. You hear the prayers I cannot even put into words. I ask You to comfort me and heal the wounds that have been opened by this hurt. Your word says in Psalm 34:18, "The Lord is close to the brokenhearted and saves those who are crushed in spirit." Father, I cling to that promise now. Draw close to me and lift up my crushed spirit.

I ask for Your strength to forgive, even when my flesh doesn't want to. I know forgiveness doesn't excuse the pain, but it frees me from bitterness. Lord, teach me to release my family member into Your hands. You are the righteous Judge, and You know their heart better than I do.

At the same time, I pray for them, Father. Whatever is broken inside of them that causes them to hurt others, heal it. Whatever wounds they carry, touch them with Your love. Remind me that they, too, are Your child in need of grace.

Give me wisdom, Lord, to know when to speak and when to stay silent, when to draw close and when to set healthy boundaries. Let my words and actions be guided by Your Spirit, not my pain. Let me walk in love but also in truth.

Most of all, Lord, remind me that You are my refuge. When family fails, You never will. When I feel unloved, Your love surrounds me. When I feel rejected, You accept me fully. Anchor me in that truth and let Your peace guard my heart in Jesus' name, I pray, Amen.

Closing Prayer

Abba Father, I have come to the end of this book, but not the end of my journey with You. I ask that every word prayed here becomes life in my heart, strength in my spirit, and power in my daily walk. Let breakthroughs be released, healing flow, and faith be restored. I trust You for the answers, Lord, and I give You glory for what is yet to come. In Jesus' mighty name, Amen

Daily Declaration Prayer

Heavenly Father,

Today I choose to bring my hurt to You instead of holding onto it. I release the pain my family member has caused me into Your hands. Strengthen me to walk in forgiveness and surround me with Your peace.

Your word says in Psalm 34:4, "I sought the Lord, and He heard me, and delivered me from all my fears." Lord, I seek You right now. Hear my cry, deliver me from fear, anger, and bitterness, and fill my heart with Your love.

Thank You that You are my refuge and healer. I rest in Your presence today in Jesus' name, Amen.

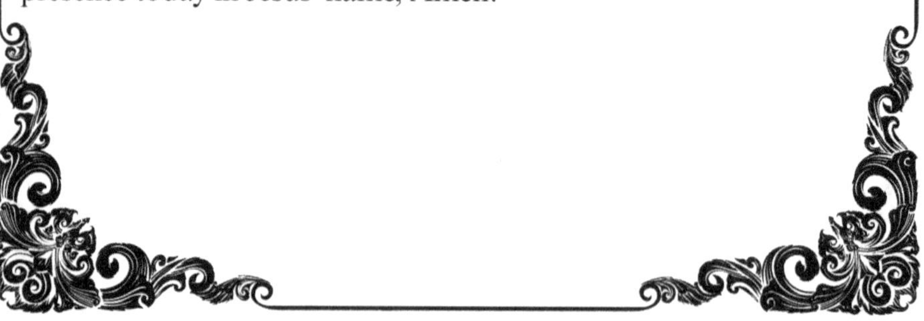

Author's Note

When I wrote this prayer book, I was not writing theory. I was writing from life, its pain, its beauty, its losses, and its miracles.
I know what it is to cry urgent prayers. I know what it is to need God's hand in the midnight hour. And I know what it is to see Him show up.

My prayer is that as you read, your faith will ignite, your heart will be encouraged, and your spirit will be renewed. Use these prayers daily, return to them when life overwhelms you, and let them become part of your journey with God.

Remember, prayer is never wasted. Every word you pray is heard. Every tear you cry is seen. And every urgent prayer rises before the throne of a faithful God who loves you.
With love,

Charma-Lee Ritchie

Epilogue

As you have journeyed through these one hundred urgent prayers, may you have felt the nearness of God's Spirit and the assurance that your voice matters in Heaven. Every cry of the heart, whether whispered in silence or poured out in tears, is heard by the One who loves without measure.

This book was not written merely to be read, but to be lived. Each prayer represents the struggles, the joys, the doubts, and the victories that make up the fabric of our lives. My prayer is that these words inspire you to continue seeking God in the raw moments of life, when your strength feels gone and when hope seems out of reach.

Always remember: the urgency of your prayer is not in the perfection of your words, but in the sincerity of your heart. The Father leans in close when His children call.

As you close this book, may you step into a deeper awareness that you are never alone. The God of restoration, healing, and breakthrough walks beside you. Let these prayers be the spark that ignites your faith anew, reminding you that with God, nothing is impossible.

For readers who desire a deeper, more personal prayer experience, this book can be beautifully paired with the Prayer Journal for Women. While Urgent Prayers gives voice to what is on the heart, the journal provides space to reflect, listen, and respond. Designed as a guided companion, it invites you to write your prayers, meditate on Scripture, and document your spiritual journey over time. Together, the prayer book and journal create a more intentional rhythm of prayer one that moves beyond reading into relationship, helping you connect with God not only through spoken words, but through thoughtful reflection and written devotion.

Available on Amazon

For men who want to engage prayer with greater intention and clarity, this book can be paired with the Prayer Journal for Men. While Urgent Prayers helps articulate heartfelt petitions before God, the journal offers structured space to reflect, write, and discern His direction. Designed as a guided companion, it encourages men to process Scripture, record prayers, and document spiritual growth with honesty and purpose. Together, the prayer book and journal foster a more disciplined and meaningful prayer life, one that strengthens faith, sharpens spiritual awareness, and deepens a man's personal walk with God.

Available on Amazon

www.ingramcontent.com/pod-product-compliance
Lightning Source LLC
Chambersburg PA
CBHW072233150726
48002CB00005B/2073